Conquer Trauma Drama: Breakthrough Curriculum

Conquer Trauma Drama: Breakthrough Curriculum

Jo Standing

The author of this book does not dispense medical advice or prescribe the use of any technique as a form of treatment for physical, mental, or emotional problems without the advice of a physician, either directly or indirectly. The intent of the author is only to offer information and entertainment to help you in your quest for emotional, mental, physical and spiritual well-being. In the event you use any of the information in this book for yourself, which is your constitutional right, the author, the publisher and all mentioned herein assume no responsibility for your actions.

For additional enquiries, contact Jo Standing and Team at www.JoStanding.com.
To book the author to speak at your next event, lead workshops, classes, or programs with your business, not-for-profit or favorite social group please contact the author directly at www.JoStanding.com.

ISBN-13: 9781548449704
ISBN-10: 1548449709

Conquer Trauma Drama Breakthrough Curriculum is used in both paid programs at www.JoinTheUnbound.com aka www.OurVetCommunnity.com as well as in free programs given by The Viva Standing Foundation. The VSF is a government recognized 501(c)3 not-for-profit and is designed to offer workshops, classes, programs, educational materials, symposiums, talks and forums to inspire survivors of rape and war to thrive after the fact. For more information visit www.VivaStanding.org

TABLE OF CONTENTS

Foreword

Jessica Knoll, author of the bestselling novel, *Luckiest Girl Alive,* in an interview recounting the most terrible scenes from her novel, based in large part on her true life experience at the age of fifteen, states: "I was so conditioned to not talk about that (her gang raped by three young men), it did not occur to me to be forthcoming." Likewise, the young boys that were sexually assaulted and abused by Boston area Catholic priests, as depicted in the 2015 Academy Award winning movie, *Spotlight,* carried the shame and trauma of their experience well into their adult lives, until *Boston Globe* reporters managed to get them to talk about their experiences. Had they had the benefit of *Jo Standing's* book these victims and others like them might have had the necessary opportunity to heal from the experiences they underwent in a gentle, thorough and supportive manner as is the way with *The Breakthrough Curriculum.*

This book is a much-needed contribution to individuals who have been unable to speak openly about the unspeakable things they have suffered. Through thought-provoking questions and simple self-discovery exercises, to be practiced individually or with friends, family members or a support group, each chapter of this book offers victims of traumatic experiences a real opportunity to process their hurt and remedy the scars that have affected their bodies, minds, and ultimately their souls.

The Breakthrough Curriculum encourages the very thing that most traumatized victims need the most: an opportunity to self-evolve from victim to a healed survivor and victor and is a seamless companion to Jos-Madelaine's paperback, *Conquer Trauma Drama: Get Your Life Back,* with each individual page dedicated to each chapter within the paperback. For those seeking to heal from their traumatic hurts, *Conquer Trauma Drama: Get Your Life Back* and *Conquer Drama Trauma: The Workbook* should be read in tandem and treasured as valuable self-recovery tools.

Thomas DiGrazia
Former Adjunct Professor of Mediation and Conflict at Hawaii Pacific University
Author of *Light On Peacemaking (2016) and Peacemaker: A Sicilian-American Memoir* (2013)
Foreword written in April 2016

Introduction

***To be successful* in the reading of this book you will want to remember that you are in control of how fast or slow you move through the questions and exercises.** You are free to learn at your own pace as this is your own journey. Whether you take the online programs or not this book grants you the opportunity to start meaningful conversations with friends, family, neighbors and community members at your local cafe, community center or anywhere else you strike up a conversation! In the event that you like the idea of meeting new people then the online programs held via webcast and phone are for you!

This book is in direct correlation to the paperback, *Conquer Trauma Drama: Get Your Life Back.* You may reference the chapters of the paperback as you go through this book. It is up to you whether you start this book from beginning to end, or jump around from chapter to chapter in your process. It is best to set aside a specific amount of time to sit with each of the worksheets. **Also, try not to do more than (2) sheets per day** so that the accumulated self-knowledge that you are building has time to fully sink-in and integrate into your ever changing life. **By the end of this book**, the author suspects that you will have a momentous shift of self-awareness, a newfound sense of encouragement, and the motivation to change, shift and reshape your life to best align with your vision of who you are today and who you want to become in the upcoming days, weeks, months and years!

This book is appropriate for readers eighteen years of age and up unless otherwise permitted by the guardian and/or supervisor of those eighteen and younger.

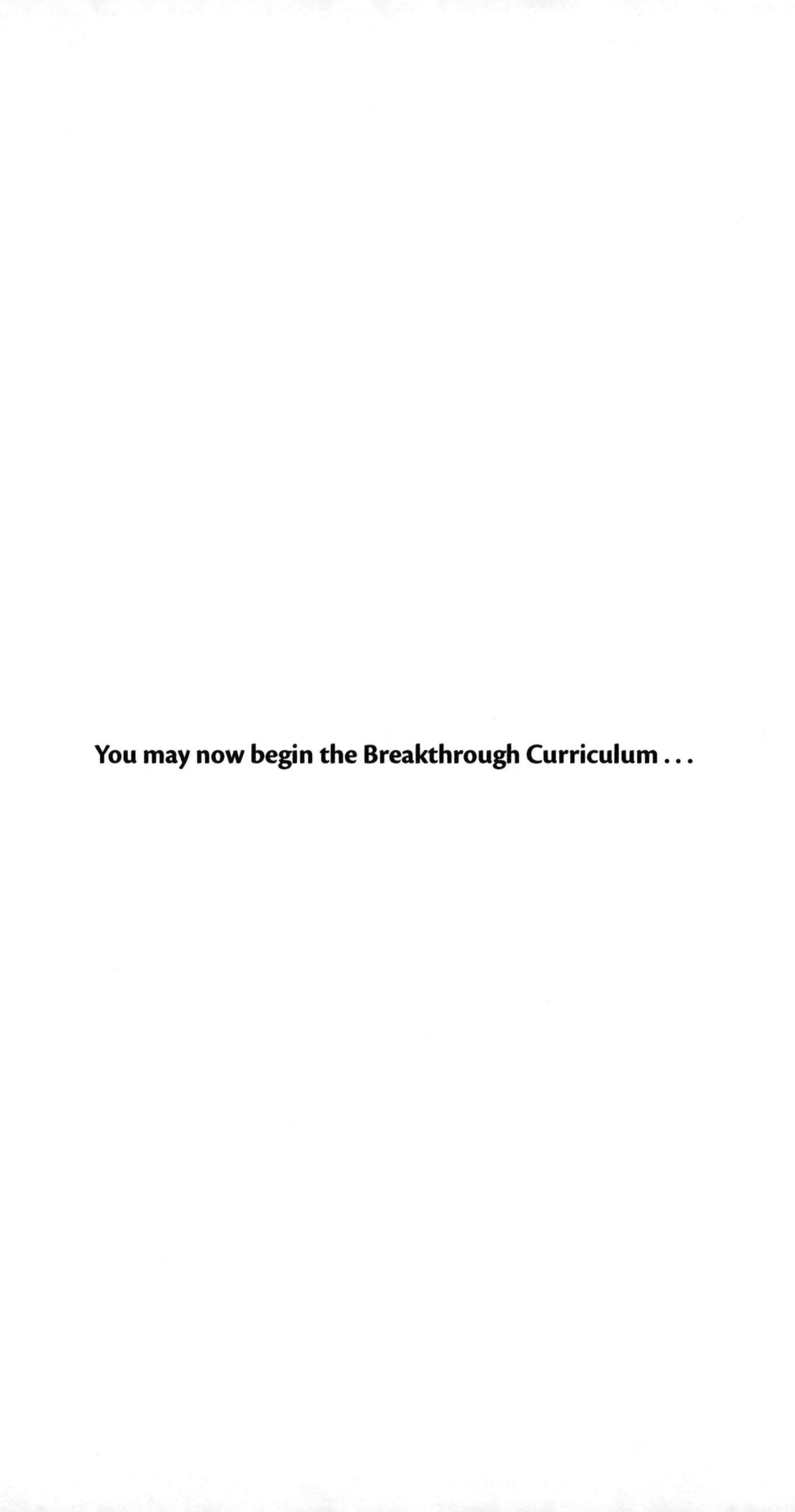

You may now begin the Breakthrough Curriculum . . .

For this sheet, Reference the Introduction of Conquer Trauma Drama: Get Your Life Back

Fun Fact: It is key to write your answers by hand and not by computer. This will improve your connection to your healing and empowerment process and increase the likelihood of your success on your path to wellness. As quoted by The Guardian, "Pens and keyboards bring into play very different cognitive processes. 'Handwriting is a complex task which requires various skills – feeling the pen and paper, moving the writing implement, and directing movement by thought,' says Edouard Gentaz, professor of developmental psychology at the University of Geneva." The Guardian article goes to say, "Drawing each letter by hand substantially improves subsequent recognition," Neuroscientist Gentaz explains.

Questions:

1) Think of a time when you experienced a trauma that was of an emotional nature although physically you were unharmed. Be unbiased. **Write down the very first thing that comes to mind.**
2) What is your go to when feeling detached from life, in general, as a byproduct of being overwhelmed by a challenging experience? Is it a feeling? An action? An activity? A behavior? A person? Or, a mix of all of these? **Write down what you observe** as your response to hardship, and the detached numbness that potentially occurs from being overwhelmed.
3) What is your general attitude to the people around you after you have experienced something life-challenging? How do you prefer for people to interact with you when you are being heavily challenged by life's events? **Write down your answer.**

Exercise:

You will need to find one person to work with for this part of the worksheet. If you are reading this book outside of attending a class with the *Trauma Drama Coaching Institute* then perhaps ask a friend, family member or someone you trust to join you in this exercise. Next, begin to practice the following statements with your partner. Practice taking turns saying the following sentences:

Tell me about trauma.

Tell me about your relationship to trauma.

Tell me about the support you want.

Alternate asking one another for the duration of ten minutes. This exercise is all about unearthing the unspoken by learning to go beyond the surface of conversation. Moving beyond your normal train of thought is crucial to breakthrough in order to discover your innate abilities and your resilience during traumatic time.

Your Notes:

FOR THIS SHEET, REFERENCE CHAPTER 1 OF CONQUER TRAUMA DRAMA

Get Your Life Back - What is Trauma?

Noted Fact: The National Institute of Mental Health notes that, "Some factors that increase risk for PTSD include: Having little or no social support after the event." It is therefore crucial that whether or not you already have PTSD symptoms including but not limited to loss of appetite or compulsive eating, problems sleeping, anxiety or depression that you push beyond your comfort zone and find a free or paid option to sit, walk, march, dance, play or in some way join people in your community. Any activity that practices moderation and healthy, wholesome, engagement is an asset to rebuilding connection to your positive self.

Questions:

1) When you think of the word trauma what are the first things, images or understandings that come to mind?
2) How do you usually respond when you have learned someone you know and care about has experienced something traumatic? There is no 'wrong' or 'right' answer here. This is a learning experience that can only enrich your life if you are honest and as clear as possible with your answers.
3) What forms of support do you think are most necessary in order to heal?
4) What encourages you to want to heal?
5) What have you found has absolutely ***not*** supported you to breakthrough the struggles of trauma and its effects? What can you do about that?

Exercise:

Please get a pen and paper and turn on your television, or *Netflix on your computer.* Locate the first show or video that you wish to begin with for this exercise. Dedicate 20-30 minutes to viewing the show in front of you. **Write down** each time that you notice a character, or real life person being filmed, is experiencing something traumatic. What are the traumatic events that you notice are occurring? Or, ask your friends and family to join you for the exercise. Without telling one another what each one of you are writing or noticing about the show(s), ask them to also play the game of observing... it can be interesting to see how different people interpret different events! Perhaps one person sees a traumatic experience where you did not. **For example,** being publicly humiliated, or losing sight of your beloved pet for a moment. This is a great way to get to learn more about your loved ones to greater levels than ever before.

Your Notes:

FOR THIS PAGE, REFERENCE CHAPTER 2 OF CONQUER TRAUMA DRAMA

Get Your Life Back - What is Trauma Drama?

Fun Fact: The University of California published a PDF online that start with, "Two of the most common causes of drama is misinterpretation and misunderstanding." Viatcheslav Wlassoff, Ph.D. writes in the publication Brain Blogger, "Understanding how PTSD alters brain chemistry is critical to empathize [with those suffering with PTSD]." The doctor also goes on to define the major changes in the trauma affected brain, and how our reality can be distorted based upon these changes. These involuntary modifications to the brain that occur after trauma of course can likely lead to misinterpretation and misunderstanding, for the trauma survivor, when alone as well as between the trauma survivor and other people in their lives. Wlassoff says, "The hippocampus, the ventromedial prefrontal cortex, and the amygdala complete the neural circuitry of stress." And goes into further detail within the article outlined in the resources part of this book as to how the lack of communication and connection between these brain regions can challenge the trauma survivor. However, the doctor also says, "The brain is a finely-tuned instrument. It is fragile, but it is heartening to know that the brain also has an amazing capacity to regenerate." Life is possible after trauma!

Questions:

1) What is your definition of unnecessary drama?
2) How do you normally remove yourself from drama? What else might you try as an alternative?
3) **After reading Chapter 2 of *Conquer Trauma Drama: Get Your Life*** can you think of a time when you were simply being dramatic for the playfulness and fun of it? Such as expressively singing an emotional song or using a tone of voice that is theatrically dramatic to playfully communicate a point to someone? **On the contrary,** can you think of a time when you felt as if the drama in your life was out of control and it was draining you? **Write your remarks, answers and reflections here:**

Exercise:

Write (3) of your most life-affecting experiences down with pen and paper that were at least 6 months ago. Now, ask yourself a gut-reaction feeling. Meaning, do not look for a long-winded, thorough, educated answer on behalf of your life just yet. Instead, ask yourself, am I still affected by any of the three major life events that I have listed here in an adverse way? Now, that you've asked yourself that question, **Pause.** Start at the top of your list. **Ask yourself aloud if you are still affected** by the first event listed of the three that you've written down.

Simply write yes or no. *If you find this too challenging,* enroll a supportive friend to answering the question with kinesiology muscle testing. If you have not yet tried muscle testing, then type this link into your web browser for more information. **http://tinyurl.com/CDSelfMuscleTest**

Your Notes:

FOR THIS PAGE, REFERENCE CHAPTER 3 OF CONQUER TRAUMA DRAMA

Get Your Life Back - Transforming Our Response to Trauma

Fun Fact: A magazine article in The Scientific American quotes, *"Although the brain is most pliable early in life, [when we are babies and children] "what's really new this decade is the widespread appreciation, realization and exploitation of adult plasticity."* Therefore, our ability to consciously choose what we observe and therefore highlight in our personal reality is indeed a choice. Author of many books including, *Think and Grow Rich,* Napoleon Hill says, "First comes thought; then organization of that thought, into ideas and plans; then transformation of those plans into reality. The beginning, as you will observe, is in your imagination." So, then as you work through this sheet insist that you do not stop at what you realize to be true in regards to the past but entice yourself through imagination, and belief in your ability to craft new thoughts *and* watch those new thoughts take physical root in your own life and learn to fly.

Questions:

1) What does it mean to observe? When you are observing something in your life what are you doing? What do you notice about yourself in the moment of observation?
2) What things do you most commonly observe in your romantic life? What is one thing you want to do about it?
3) What things do you most commonly observe in your work life? What is one thing you want to do about it?
4) What things do you most commonly observe in your social life? What is one thing you want to do about it?
5) There is a saying, "If you are capable of observing your thoughts then who or *"what"* is it that is observing your thoughts?" So, therefore the mind has different facets and elements to it. *If the mind can be thinking while we are observing those very thoughts, what part of us is it that is observing?*

Let's pretend for a moment that this is our consciousness. I invite you to continue to explore the following in more depth. *Consider this:* what we are most familiar with is the well known statement that we can bring out the best in others by being the best version of ourselves. However, what we do not often consider is the following: We can only bring out in ourselves what we observe in others. If we are constantly judging other people then we will, without meaning to, be highlighting those errors in ourselves, too. We cannot cast blame and judgment on others without bringing those same qualities that we dislike in others out in ourselves, too.

Exercise:

- With your pen and paper in hand next time you are "pissed off" "perturbed" or "angered" about someone else's behavior write down the exact judgement words you heard from them **and** the exact judgment words you hold about this individual.
- In the right hand column of your page quickly write the very opposite adjectives you have used to affirm about the other person. Now, below this **write in I AM sentences the words on the left and the right and conclude the full sentence with, "...and that's ok."** This includes the "negative" and the "positive", the "light" and "dark." (We must learn to love all parts of ourselves and this is a great time to practice.)

Note: We are many things as people. We cannot always be smart, or beautiful or loved by others. So, the sooner we can neutralize our judgment the sooner we can thrive by focusing on our strengths.

- Finally, write a new I AM sentence below the neutral I AM sentence:

- For example: "I am" . . . then fill in the adjectives that you have written above on the right hand side that highlight the potential of your humanity and your possibilities of greatness within. Complete the sentence with the "why" by adding the word "because ____________________." (Fill in the blank with why you believe this to be so.

Why are you great?
Essentially, we alleviate our suffering by forgiving the judgments we have about ourselves. Oftentimes, if not always, judgments from others are a reflection of judgments we have stored within *ourselves about ourselves.* Therefore it is us who is the real catalyst for change. Now, get writing!

Your Notes:

FOR THIS PAGE, REFERENCE CHAPTER 4 OF CONQUER TRAUMA DRAMA

Get Your Life Back - How to Become a Novice of Your Own Experience

Fun Fact: In a New York University Center for Neural Science online publication Joseph E. LeDoux writes, *"There is much to be learned about the non-emotional, non- conscious ingredients that contribute to conscious feelings."* One might wonder what is meant by this. Do you? For the completion of this sheet, consider your body feelings, your inside feelings felt within, and your outwardly expressed emotions, as you explore the questions. [*Note: See Resources for a link to more of the publication mentioned in this fact finding.*]

Questions:

1) Please begin by writing down a trauma that you feel is **most relevant to your life right now** due to observing miniature versions of it reappearing in your life from time to time. **Write down what the past experience that you've identified as a trauma was *in as few words as possible.*** *Try to stick to one sentence maximum.*
2) Write exactly what happened in the trauma that you've listed in number one **minus any judgments about the situation or the people involved.** Only write the step-by-step actions that created the experience of the original trauma.
3) Next, write the **feelings that you personally had** about the trauma.
4) Reviewing the details in number one, two and three **think about and write down** ways you might **physically** express the feelings that the moment of trauma held for you.

For example: Some possible options might be to go to rock climbing, boxing, or to the local arts and crafts store to purchase acrylics, and a canvas, and paint without any idea of what you might paint. In this case, just allow the brush to do the work while your favorite music plays in the background. **Allow** feelings to be expressed through the physical act of painting, climbing, boxing, or whatever else you might prescribe yourself as the best conscious physical activity. You might choose to play a variety of emotionally-charged music, close the door to a private space where you can be alone, and allow your body to move to the sound of the music that you select that mirrors the physical sensations you had in the moment that you have completed writing about in number one.

5) Now, once you have chosen *and enacted* your selected form of physical expression, get your notepad or journal and pen to write with and explore what it is that you are feeling in this moment.
6) Speak aloud the following affirmations: **"Today, on ______ day in ______ (write the year) I feel __________, _________ and ____________."** Now write, **"I allow myself to feel this with all my inner strength because I know that feeling is what makes me most alive and human of all things."** Finally now write, **"I am coming into this experience to fully own it, occupy it and transform it."**
7) Write down the following sentence, "I imagine that people who have experienced the event of _________ (the event described in number one) may also have the above feelings that I have just uncovered for myself."

Exercise:

Open your computer and enter the category of survivors or people described in #7 into the search engine. Google or Bing search engines are fine. Locate a story involving other people *you do not know* who have experienced the same thing you have experienced. Next, silently say a thought prayer for them. Include the above affirmations that you have said for yourself from number two. "Today, on _______________ day in _______________ (write the year) I acknowledge that this person might be feeling _______________, _____________ and _____________. I pray that these people allow themselves to feel their feelings with all their inner strength because feeling is what makes us most alive and human." Finally, now write or say this last thought prayer, "I pray they can come into their experience in order to fully own it, occupy it and transform it, from within first, just as I am."

Your Notes:

FOR THIS SHEET, REFERENCE CHAPTER 5 OF CONQUER TRAUMA DRAMA

Get Your Life Back - Drama is a Fact of Life, Like it or Not!

Fun Fact: In a recent publication, FastCompany.com notes, *"In a 2014 study conducted by Kaufman, 72% of respondents around the world* ***reported having some kind of new insight in the shower."*** So, this means that it's important to remain calm when endeavoring to do anything new. Especially, when it requires creating new worlds for ourselves to occupy in our day to day lives through the initial effort of thinking new thoughts... The following worksheet may seem superfluous and without any real weight or significance. However, approaching our lives from various angles then enables our minds to stretch more, and activates new sections in our brains, which in turn can then be applied to all areas of our lives as we move forward.

Questions:

1) **Choose** a trauma that is most relevant to the moment, either the same trauma from the last worksheet, or a different past experience from your life. **Write it down in one sentence or less.**
2) **Now,** write down the natural element that the event most symbolizes in your mind. **For example:** water, wind, fire, earth, light or space. **Note:** this is an abstract exercise. Please **choose** to think abstractly for this exercise.
3) **Handwrite,** "I most identify this particular event with the element of______________ **because** ____.
4) What element (of the ones listed above in number one) do you think the experience was lacking that might have been vital in order to help transcend the hurt associated with the event that you have experienced because of the event? **Choose water, fire, earth, wind, light or space. Write it down and describe why.** If you find this section challenging, think of times when you were creative or flexible in your thinking in the past. If you have a challenging time recollecting creative moments in your life, ask a friend or colleague for their help in recalling an

experience when you were flexible or creative. Take note of these times and write at least one supportive affirmation that states your ability to complete this worksheet.

5) Write with pen and paper, **"Today I begin to trust myself enough to be creative in the reconstruction of my life. From now on, I allow flexibility in my thinking for the purpose of experimenting where having control is most effective in my life and allocating my attention and focus in the areas that I have most control."**

Exercise:

Bring a friend, loved one, classmate or mentor into the conversation. Discuss why you agree or disagree with the above affirmation. Share any resistance that may have come up for you in the writing of the above statements. Share any feelings, triggers, or insights you may have come in contact with during the above three points of focus.

Your Notes:

FOR THIS SHEET, REFERENCE CHAPTER 6 OF CONQUER TRAUMA DRAMA

Get Your Life Back - The Top Seven Challenges of Trauma Drama

Fun Fact: The media source, Huffington Post, says, "In 2011 World Health Organization report called noise pollution a "modern plague," concluding that "there is overwhelming evidence that exposure to environmental noise has adverse effects on the health of the population." Therefore, cultivating moments in our lives by simply being open to them that are quiet is central to our overall health and best day to day functioning. Whether it be walking in a quiet neighborhood, driving in the country without music on and listening to the nature in the area, hunting for survival purposes with reverence for the animal, or something else, integrating quiet into daily life is essential for processing the newly realized ideas that are idling underneath our conscious minds and thoughts that rest in our awareness. Underneath the routine thoughts we must repeat day to day are thoughts waiting to be heard that can enrich your inner and outer wealth.

Questions:

1) **Record with pen and paper** when you notice there is usually silence in your day or evening while you are in your waking hours. **Make a note** about what happens in that silence for you.
2) Are there recurring life-limiting thoughts or feelings that arise when you are in a silent moment? **If yes, list a couple.**
3) **Next, write the exact opposite** to the life-limiting thought(s) you listed in number two. Use affirmative words that support the direction you **do,** in fact, want to go in, moving forward.
4) What do you think may, or may not happen, if you were to share the answers you have written down in number one, two and three with a friend or family member? Do you like the idea of sharing the above with anyone? Why? Or, why not?

5) How comfortable on a scale 1-10 are you to share the challenges that arise in your silent moments, as listed above, as well as the details of the direction you desire to go in as a healthy alternative? Why?

Exercise:

Invite a friend or partner into a 10-minute conversation where you intend to listen to one another, closely with undivided attention, with the intention of *only saying words that create connection.* This means, leave all spoken words out of this ten minutes that are intended to provoke *any one particular outcome.* If you do not know who may or may not be interested in this level of consciousness work, simply practice it without notifying the person that you are only speaking words with the intention to connect and not lead into any one particular direction. **You are not speaking words to question or influence the person in any way that you have chosen to work with to act or be a different way than they presently are.** Do not try and change them in any way, only receive them and meet them exactly where they are for the 10 prescribed minutes of this exercise.

Your Notes:

FOR THIS SHEET, REFERENCE CHAPTER 7 OF CONQUER TRAUMA DRAMA

Get Your Life Back - Is It OK To Live in a World of Good and Bad?

Fun Fact: In an article in Live Science, the following is reported about human memory, "Entering or exiting through a doorway serves as an 'event boundary' in the mind, which separates episodes of activity and files them away," Gabriel Radvansky, a psychologist at the University of Notre Dame, told Live Science in a 2011 interview. "Recalling the decision or activity that was made in a different room is difficult because it has been compartmentalized." Let's look at this fact as an escalation of importance on the ever changing human mind. Since much of our experience relies on how we remember and interpret our lives, past, present and future, we can then be conscious with the above information and use our intention to selectively engage our reasoning and goal setting in physical areas that most support the success of those same goals and ideas having the potential of having longevity in our lives. Then, we return to those physical areas to re-imprint our intentions. Bottomline, it is crucial to be aware of our thoughts, write them down when of significance, and return to them in supportive, intentional, environments.

Questions:

1) What were your first impressions of life that you remember? **List 3 feeling words,** and 3 general statements no longer than one sentence each to answer the question in two parts.
2) Do you tend to look at any of your life experiences as being solely 'bad'? **Answer the question by writing 'yes' or 'no'.** If yes, write 'why' you perceive a past situation as being only bad. To complete this step, write what might change in your present and/or future life if you were to locate a way to view the past event differently by seeing both strengths and weaknesses that evolved because of the past event.
3) **In this step:** create an affirmation or life-giving statement that affirms for you why this experience in the above might succeed at bringing you greater self-understanding, new realizations, hopes and possibly even future goals and successes, that may not occurred had the experience

coined as 'bad' not happened. If there is not an event you view as solely 'bad' from your past then look at writing down the first two benefits of a past trauma by the way that it has acted out in your life long term. Now, read the two sentences to yourself silently or aloud. Finally, for this step, expand on each of the individual sentences by writing one more follow-up sentence that naturally plays well with the initial sentence you wrote down. For instance, if you wrote down, "Because of my experience I am able to see life in more complexity than I used to." Then, you may follow that with, "Because I see life with more complexity I am more engaged with life as a whole and have been able to connect with and empathize with more people than I otherwise might have done."

4) Consider freedom as being happy with where you are right now. For a moment think about all the challenges that life is currently presenting as a byproduct of not having complete resolution with the 'bad' past event. **Write them down** and then follow the sentences that list the challenges with ***". . .and, that's OK. I am free to change my circumstances in any moment and I therefore fully embrace the impermanence of even this moment. "***
5) Make a list of one 'thing' you'd like to create in your life based on each of the rewards that you've found. What might you do with that knowledge?

Exercise:

As an experiment, **keep a pen and paper with you throughout the course of twenty-four hours** and document how often you or someone around reduces an experience to being merely 'good' or 'bad'. After noting what is being called simply good or bad, check-in with yourself about how you really feel about the event, circumstance or idea that is being coined as "good or bad". Intentionally give each experience or thought that is being pegged as 'good' or 'bad' two to three new adjectives. **Write the new descriptive words down.**

For example you may write something like this: "Whereas I once found/they find this as being 'bad', I now see it as more like challenging, new, bold and scary." And, then follow that with, **"And, that's OK."**

Your Notes:

FOR THIS SHEET, REFERENCE CHAPTER 8 OF CONQUER TRAUMA DRAMA

Get Your Life Back - What Do You Do with Judgment?

Fun Fact: In an article by Berkeley, the following is stated, "Science doesn't make moral judgments." This is of course true, science cannot illustrate certainties when it comes to subjective moral issues because as the saying goes, "to each his own." When we look at this we then might wonder how to quantify both the judgments we have about ourselves and others when they are held in certainty. How are we or anyone else served by holding onto to fixed ideas about anyone person? How does this do a disservice? Be gentle with yourself as you consider answering the following questions.

Questions:

1) What is the most common reaction you notice from yourself when you become aware that someone is judging you and the judgment is true to you? What are your thoughts, words, reactions? **Write them down as "I accept that up until this point my reaction has been ______________."**
2) On the flipside, what is the most common reaction you notice from yourself when you become aware that someone is judging you and the judgment is **not** true to you? What are your thoughts, words, reactions? **Write them down as "I accept that up until this point my reaction has been __________?"**
3) When you hear the expression, "Use your better judgment," What exactly do you think is meant by it? **Write down your answer.**
4) When do you notice that judgement is <u>healthy</u> in relation to your life and your thoughts? **Write down your findings.**
5) When do you notice that judgement is <u>unhealthy</u> in relation to your life and your thoughts? Write down your findings.
6) Whose opinions do you trust in your life right now? **Write your answer. Now, write why.**

Exercise:

Step 1: Ask 5-10 people in your community what they do or how they react or respond when they become instantly aware that someone is judging them negatively. Record their answers either in memory or by writing them down. **Step 2:** Write whether or not you agree with their methods. Write **WHY** you do, or do not, agree with them.

Step 3: Based on your new findings, write out a game plan for how you will choose to *respond in the future to negative judgment* and why you think it is the best approach.

Step 4: What can you do today in order to reinforce your intended mindful response?

Your Notes

FOR THIS SHEET, REFERENCE CHAPTER 9 OF CONQUER TRAUMA DRAMA

Get Your Life Back - Is It Over Yet?

Fun Fact: The Economist writes, "A simple idea underpins science: "trust, but verify"." Therefore, *all* discovery starts with *trust.* We go nowhere without it. Therefore, even at a time of great doubt mixed with seemingly inescapable life challenge we must face the situation with a refurbished belief that we are not at the *end* of our lives but instead suspect that we are standing at the door of possibility. In the following questions hold fast to your sense of curiosity and openness to the chance that you might stumble into something great and unknown.

Questions:

1) What is the longest-term challenge that you have in your life? **Write down your answer.**
2) Answer this question: How might you turn this long-term challenge listed in number one into a stage of your life so that it does not become a permanent issue? **Write stream of consciousness for a total of 5 minutes** without intending to go any one direction with your thoughts. Just write what comes to mind. Then, share the challenge you listed in number one with one person. Next, brainstorm with that person how you *might* make this challenge a valued part of your life *and no longer a nearly all-defining reality.*
3) What are your hopes for life *if and when* the long-term challenge you listed in number one is actually resolved? **Write down your answer. Next, write (2) general thoughts** that you might have run through your mind, **if** this new stage of life were to come about.

Life Tip: Real problems bring us to potential within ourselves. Made-up problems only have us going over old ground in our minds. A permanent problem is one that is incapable of being transmuted to another "stage of being," or one that never "changes form" due to various possible circumstances, although most often a permanent problem arises because one or more people are unwilling to change how they show up in the problems that one or more people have identified.

3) Can you name a permanent problem in your life? **If yes, list one.**
4) Can you name a made-up problem that you've observed in your life at any point in time? **If yes, list one.**

Next, once you have answered the above, consider that all problems have *potential.* In fact, problems bring us to a potential *within* ourselves. They always challenge us to see a different shade of ourselves or a different angle of our lives. This is only the case if we look at them with curiosity and hope combined. Remember, problems are great. *They lead to solutions!*

Exercise:

Consider why the long-term challenge that you've now explored, spoken about, and written about **might** have entered your life to begin with. If you already know why, you are invited to still do this exercise one more time for the sake of possibly uncovering more information about yourself in order to permit living a long and happy life.

Pause for a minute: as you close your eyes consider how long the list might be **if** you were to think about all the reasons **why** this challenge occurred in your life. Is that imaginary list long? Or, is it short with emotionally-heavy, and loaded reasons as to why the event(s) happened in your life?

For a moment, consider all the energy that just went into <u>merely considering</u> writing the list. ***PLEASE DO NOT ACTUALLY WRITE THE LIST,** just <u>imagine</u> writing the list.*

Now, put pen to paper and begin writing <u>why and how you have grown</u> since the event or events occurred that had created and/or constructed your long-term challenge.

Remember from the book *Conquer Trauma Drama: Get Your Life Back*. . .they did not happen "to" you. . . ***They happened.*** Period. **And . . . You *experienced* them.**

Your Notes

FOR THIS SHEET, REFERENCE CHAPTER 10 OF CONQUER TRAUMA DRAMA

Get Your Life - The Top Challenges of Trauma

Fun Fact: We all have our challenges. *It's part of life!* In fact, when The Atlantic writes in an article, "We realize with a jolt that what we perceive is never the world directly, but rather our brain's best guess at what that world is like. . ." it directly points to the fact that even our perception of the world is through an individual filter that doesn't necessarily reflect the truth of the world we live in. This means that as a human challenges are almost inevitable because our very nature is that we are constantly trying to get the external world to match our internal world and vice versa. As we know, that is not always possible, at least not immediately, or on an ongoing basis. Therefore, embrace your challenges and get ready to explore them in this next worksheet!

Questions:

1) Based off of the top six challenges listed within **Chapter 10 of Conquer Trauma Drama: Get Your Life Back,** what is the top challenge of the six listed in the book that you are presently most affected by in your day to day life? **Write your answer here.**
2) **Write 3 ways why the challenge is real for you.** How do you know the challenge exists in your life? Please list your answer(s) here.
3) **Next, follow the above answers with the spoken and handwritten words,** *"And, that's okay . . . because I love and approve of myself always in all ways. I allow myself to be as I am while striving to integrate all of my life experiences for a complete and NEW me."*
4) **Handwrite, "I have found ____________ (include the top challenge in the blank) *difficult in the past* <u>and</u> I realize that even a second ago <u>is the past.</u> This new moment and *this new breath* is my key to granting me fresh introspection and a new experience that best suits who I am today. I have an unlimited center of power within me at all times. I rely on my OWN validation as I make progress in MY life toward great inner freedom."** Keep this sentence in a place where you will easily revisit it. You may write this sentence more than

once if you are wanting to amplify the outcome. Make sure to write longhand and do not type. Remember, the writing of letters by hand increases the engagement of the brain.

5) **Next write a life-giving sentence.** For Example: if you write or say, "It is difficult for me to allow life to happen because I am afraid of what might happen if I give it all my effort." **Then, your flip statement might be,** "I gracefully allow life to move within me, and around me, and I myself to flow within life itself, because I know that I am a divine creator who has power to influence what I desire most in my life."

Exercise:

Read the two paragraphs titled, "It's Time" on page 74 of Conquer Trauma Drama: Get Your Life Back. Next, watch the free *TEDX* video online by Brene Brown entitled, *The Power of Vulnerability.* Next, choose a friend or someone you know through a mutual healing or empowerment-focused local or online class and ask them if you may speak with them about the work you're doing in this Workbook. Keep asking until you find someone you can share with. Share this exercise with them by telling them about your greatest challenge with facing the aftereffects of trauma and also how you are learning to shift with your new self-prescribed power statement aka affirmation. Finally, invite them to do the same. If they accept your invitation, walk them through the steps of this worksheet with a friendly and caring demeanor without validating or disqualifying anything they say or see to be true. Thank them for sharing. Make sure to set a time boundary around how much time you have to listen.

Your Notes

FOR THIS SHEET, REFERENCE CHAPTER 11 OF CONQUER TRAUMA DRAMA

Get Your Life Back - Are You Accidentally Creating Drama In Your Life?

Fun Fact: Jo Standing, the author of this breakthrough curriculum believes that the aversion or resistance to feeling one's own pain is the exact source of all unnecessary, frivolous or shallow drama, that occurs between people in day to day life. In an article, Live Science observes pain as such, "Pain is a complex mixture of emotions, culture, experience, spirit and sensation." So much is yet to be known about pain or where it comes from. The publication Scientific American says, "Anger and sadness are an important part of life, and new research shows that experiencing and accepting such emotions are vital to our mental health." We as individuals or collectively cannot abate pain if we are seeing our feelings as being negative or if we are running away from facing our lives' natural occurrence of pain. Consider yourself a courageous warrior as you explore the below thoughts in this worksheet.

Questions:

1) What is pain to you?
2) How does pain challenge you?
3) What value, if any, does pain have in your life?
4) What place does pain have in your life right now?
5) How do you currently experience pain in your body? Your mind? Your feelings? Your emotions? Write one example for each aspect of you aka mind, body, feelings, emotions.
6) What do you think pain's function is in your life right now? Or, what do you think it might be trying to teach you?
7) **Handwrite the following nonviolent note to pain.** "Dear Pain, I thank you for being in my life at this moment. I see your use and function in my life. I am open to learning how to embrace you so that I may then begin to heal fully and **live** my life to it's fullest. Pain, what is it that I may do to embrace you more fully so that you may be felt, heard and seen? How is it best for me to

do this as a simple exercise in my day to day life that will only take a few minutes at most?" If you have an idea to the question then write it here. **Otherwise, simply handwrite the statement as seen here** as a way to connect to the possibility that you might positively trigger a future thought and solution to the question contained within this handwritten section.

Exercise

Step 1: Keep your journal or a loose leaf folded piece of paper with you at all times for the next 48-hours. When you find yourself upset about circumstances that are outside of the immediate physical reality that you are in write both the exact thought(s) that are of distress as well as any mental visual or the picture in your mind that occurs at the same time as the thought(s).

Quickly jot your discovery down in a few brief descriptive words.

Step 2: Prepare for this step by closing your eyes partly or all the way at the next rest break you have. Take two full belly breaths. Feel your feet on the floor. Get grounded, centered and calm through your breath. Focus on any picture that may have been connected to the source of upset that is presently **not** in your physical surroundings that you may have identified in **Step 1.**

Step 3: With your eyes either partly or all the way closed now imagine enlarging that photo or picture in your mind until you can't make it any larger and then "blow it up", into sparkling, non-threatening, "confetti-looking" pieces. Imagine the picture that was once seemingly harmful now vanishing from your mind's eye.

Take two more breaths for this exercise and as you do so **imagine a pristine, calm, and favorable environment** that you benefit from on all levels, including emotionally, mentally, spiritually and physically. Focus on your chosen environment for five to ten more breaths to complete this exercise.

Pause for a moment after practicing this exercise for the first time. Realize that you've just given yourself new space inside of yourself where you were formerly experiencing the life-limiting experience. Consider saying the following statement to yourself, *"At this time, for now, I am ok. And, if or when I need to return to the thoughts or visual I was experiencing before I can do so if it serves to provide greater clarity or knowing within."* You may also try practicing this thought, *"All details are taken care of and I now allow my mind, heart, body and soul to focus on this moment's top priority. This moment's top priority is*

______________________.

Your Notes

FOR THIS SHEET, REFERENCE CHAPTER 12 OF CONQUER TRAUMA DRAMA

Get Your Life Back - Living As A Negative Result

Fun Fact: Berkeley University of California states, "Years of research suggests that empathy and social intelligence are vastly more important to acquiring and exercising power than are force, deception, or terror." The study shows that the humane way people acquire power is oftentimes eroded by the actualization of the obtainment and experience of power. This leads us to see that we as people might become what we are not in the false idea that we need to be something else in order to maintain our sense of power. Thoughtfulness, kindness, a genuine interest in others are all traits and ways of being that determine whether or not we maintain the internal sense that we are worthwhile in the world from our own felt sense. Therefore, when we keep ourselves in check by noting how we might have screwed up in a situation we access the feelings that guarantee we both feel and see our lives from a powerful and healthy life-giving perspective. As you do the below questions, maintain healthy emotions toward yourself, as you explore possible alternative actions and reactions, and identify past choices.

Questions:

1) Think of a time when you have altered your behavior in a negative way in reaction to someone else's behavior. **Jot down your answer.** Next, was your *negative reaction* planned or unplanned? **Write down your answer.**
2) What caused your negative reaction in that moment? Answer the question by observing the changes within yourself as well as the external triggering factors. **Write your answer.**
3) Focusing on the event that you have conjured up in your memory in number one, list one or more ways that your reaction to the event was life-limiting.
4) What did it (the negative reaction) give life to that might be transferable to the developing of a skill that you have had or might want to have in the future?

Exercise:

Further reinforce your strengths by designing a new affirmation to practice:

Note: The word 'arbitrator' is an example. Write your own skill, talent or gift in the blank: "I am aware that I am a great arbitrator and I see and know deeply that I am capable of integrating that _______ into my life on a regular basis in order to benefit many people in addition to myself. I realize that I am blessed to have my natural skills, gifts and talents. And, I plan on growing and expanding them strategically with each passing day. My next step to continuing to grow this positive ability that I've listed here in my life is _____________." I commit to doing that _________ (write when you plan on committing to the action step you've listed in the previous blank).

Your Notes

FOR THIS SHEET, REFERENCE CHAPTER 13

How Can I Help?

Fun Fact: In the process of learning how to love we must learn how to equally love ourselves as we do others. A study backs this opinion as seen in Huffington Post, *"Research published in the journal Health Psychology found that building yourself up instead of tearing yourself down can lead to better health decisions."* In fact, TIME also says, *"People often think that they are motivated by self-criticism, but a burgeoning area of research suggests the opposite. Being kind to yourself, as opposed to tearing yourself down, leads to fewer bad feelings and, in turn, healthier actions."* This said, sometimes we feel it easier to love another whether it be accomplished by doing something kind for your neighbor, or family member, or volunteering. Oftentimes, this outward action of lovingkindness manifests a deep feeling of inner well-being and appreciation. Remember, in answering the below that there are no right or wrong answers when it comes to exploring what is presently true for you or has been true for your in the past.

Questions:

1) Write down what it means to care for yourself in this moment. **Include (1) answer for each body, mind, and emotional self. Write your answers here.**
2) What is one way that you might challenge your spiritual self today? **Write your answer here.**
3) Write down what it means to care for the people in your life. **Include (3) ways that caring can show up in your answer here.**
4) Write down what it means to care for the general public people who are not in your inner circle but that you might cross on a day to day or perhaps only once. **Include your answer here.**
5) Do you find it more challenging to nurture and care for yourself than it is to do so for others? **Or, vice versa,** do you find it more challenging to care for and nurture others than it is to care for yourself? **Write down your answer and include your why.**
6) In what areas of your life are you comfortable accepting and receiving help in? Why is this the case? **Write your answer.**
7) What do you think it is **not** ok to accept help with? How do you figure this to be the case? **Write your answer.**
8) When was the last time you offered to help someone without being asked? **Write your answer.**

9) In a time of need, what do you most want people to **say** to you? What do you most want people to **do**? **Write your answer in positive words.**
10) On the contrary, what do you most **NOT** want people to say and do? **Write your answer.**
11) How might you phrase this request to others?
12) What is your experience of asking for help in the past?
13) Can you think of a time when offering to be of help to someone went over well? **Write your answer here.** What did that look like? How did it feel? What is at least one thing (general idea/ belief) that you might have carried forward from that experience?
14) Think of a time when you really, deeply, appreciated receiving help from someone. **Describe that experience in 1-3 sentences.**

Exercise:

Step 1: Make a list of 5 solutions that you might be willing to welcome in your life at this time in answer to five challenges that you are currently aware of having in your life.

Step 2: Think of a loved one in need and then list 5 solutions you think **they** *might* be keen on welcoming in *their* life.

Final Action Step: Consider, *and if possible,* be of service to yourself and/or others who are in need. It is suggested to check in with them *first* **BEFORE** taking any action to be of service to others. *Make sure there is a desired need for it* before taking any action.

Your Notes

FOR THIS SHEET, REFERENCE CHAPTER 14 OF CONQUER TRAUMA DRAMA

Get Your Life Back - Embracing the Pause

Fun Fact: This worksheet is considering your life more deeply than you might on any given day. Therefore, it is crucial that you limit your attention to going other places as you focus on the following questions. *Newsweek* wrote an article called, *The Science of Making Decisions,* it says, "With too much information, people's decisions make less and less sense." According to Angelika Dimoka, director of the Center for Neural Decision Making at Temple University, info-paralysis is real, well and very much alive! So, use this awareness to empower your choices to lead you to the ability to focus on the next few sentences that you've invested your time and energy into completing!

Questions:

1) What in your own life do you have control over? Write your answers in an affirmative tone. **For example,** "I have control over how I approach things in life." **Write at least five "things" you have control over whether they be mental or body choices.**
2) Describe your relationship to change. In general, are you drawn to change? If yes, in what areas are you *most* drawn to change in your life right now? **Write your answers.**
3) When was the last time you made a change in your life, whether small or large, that was suggested by someone else? What was the outcome? Did your general relationship to change become different after that? **Write down your answer.**
4) How do you best integrate change? What activities or factors support your well-being in the midst of much needed change? **Write down your answer.**

Exercise:

Set the intention to pause in between your day's events. Pause before walking or getting into your transportation to work. Pause before beginning to cook your favorite meal of the day. Take an intentional deep breath in that moment and observe **if,** in the back of your mind, you are thinking about anything else in that moment *besides the task at hand.* **If yes,** *and it has value to you in the grand scheme of things,* please **write it down. Then, set the intention to return to it at another time.** Throughout the day, *pause...* Breathe with awareness of the *quality* of breath, check the back of your mind. Is there "gold" in the depths of your consciousness? If yes, write the valuable thoughts down in 1 or 2 words so that you may remember to grow one idea at a time!

Your Notes

FOR THIS SHEET, REFERENCE CHAPTER 15

Learning to Live the Experience

Fun Fact: What controls your free will? Or, does nothing control your free will and only you can do that? The following is not necessarily an answer but a deeper exploration of the question. In Live Science one isolated situation is recalled where more scientists than not determined that free will is nothing but an illusion because all decisions and life choices are based on the result of the individual's genetic blueprint formed by the individual's past experiences. In this article titled, "Is Free Will an Illusion?" the fighting opinion against this view is, "free will is perfectly compatible with the discoveries of neuroscience." Is it possible that the functions of free will or lack thereof are a combination of both scenarios in the human field depending on many additional circumstances? Feel free to ponder and weigh-in after you've completed the below questions!

Questions:

1) In your opinion, what is the difference between healthy resistance in your life, and unhealthy resistance, as it shows up in your life right now? **Write your answer down.**
2) What is it that you have resistance to in your life right now? Is it looking for a new job? Changing your career? Being open to new relationships? Travel? Education? Or, a number of other things? **Please write down your answer.**
3) What might you say to a friend who is resisting change even though they know it is in their best interest? **Write down your answer.**
4) What might you want a friend to say to you if the tables were reversed? **Write your answer down.**
5) Within your daily schedule, what "things" are you most drawn to doing and what "things" do you resist the most? **Write your answers down. List between 2-5 for each of the things that you are *drawn to most* and *resist the most.***
6) On a scale of 1-10 **how much do you want to change this current disposition** in regards to what you are finding as being easy to do and not easy to do? **Just write the answer to appear as the number that fits best for your reply.**

7) How healthy for you are the things that you have listed as being readily accessible to your willpower? **List one or two ways that they are either healthy or unhealthy.**

Exercise:

Sit with 1-3 other people and practice each saying this statement to one another, *"Tell me about your fate."* Make sure not to praise or reject their answer by saying things like, *"Oh, that's great!"* Or, *"That's a little strange... I've never heard that before!"* **As a listener simply say, "Thank you."** When the speaker is finished sharing. **For the speaker,** say **"Done"** when you are complete in your sharing.

For the people who are sharing in the moment, make sure to list **(1)** central focus as your answer **with a maximum of (4) supportive sentences** for the central answer you have given. *If you are reading and working through this workbook on your own,* then simply write down the statement, with one central focus and four supporting sentences for each answer that you write down. *Both are great!*

If you are in a group, you also want to make sure you are not the person who can't stop talking. You want to remember that the people you are practicing with deserve their opportunity to share, too. When the speaker is finished, make sure to say, **"I am complete in my sharing now."** Or, simply, **"Done."**

Now, say to the next participant whose turn it is, *"Tell me about your fate."*

Also, for people doing this in group, make sure when you are speaking not to refer to possibilities with the words, 'should' 'could' 'would.' If someone says that, do not interrupt them in their sharing. Simply make a mental note of it and ask that person at the end if you may comment on part of their sharing. If they are not ready to hear feedback and say, "No, thank you." Or, "I am not ready to receive any comments right now," then do **not** proceed to tell them. Respect their process. We are all growing at our own pace and we thrive most when people around us honor our rate of growth.

Your Notes

FOR THIS SHEET, REFERENCE CHAPTER 16

Chill the Frick Out, Self-Punishment: Finding Your Turning Point

Fun Fact: In the article, "The Science of Happiness" in a Harvard publication, the author talks about the professional jargon that was most repeatedly used at a recent speakers' summit. The last word the author uses in this list of most commonly used words, is 'Joy'. The author says, "*. . . and 'even' joy,*" in his recollection of the experience. It is obvious that the use of the word joy, on such a repeated basis, and in a professional setting, was a bit of a phenomenon in the author's mind. The article goes onto talk about the fact that Freud was seen to have formalized the viewpoint that all humans are, "troubled creatures in need of repair." The Harvard article touches on the Positive Psychology movement, as spearheaded by Martin Seligman, by saying that, "positive psychologists recommend focusing on people's strengths and virtues as a point of departure." As you continue to explore the many shades of your humanity, in the following questions, it is suggested that you recall the virtuous traits that prompted you to get up this morning, as well as to agree to complete this breakthrough curriculum. *Enjoy!*

Questions:

1) Can you think of a time when you had no control of external circumstances and things did not go the way you wanted? **Write down the first answer that comes to mind.**
2) What was your knee jerk reaction? Or, on the contrary, what was your calculated, thoughtful, response? **Write down your answer.**
3) On a scale of 1-10 how happy, or unhappy, were you with this response or reaction? Regardless if you were happy or unhappy with your chosen action or nonaction what *might* you do differently today if encountering those same circumstances? **Write down your answers.**
4) Do you recall what your internal dialogue was when that situation unfolded? **If yes, write it down. If no, imagine what it might have been and write it down.**
5) What was realized about it? What was unrealized about it? **Write down your answer.**
6) What do you find helps you shift out of self-defeating dialogue?

7) Is there a plotline, in your life story that you most often tell people upon meeting them? What is it? **Write it down in a paragraph or less.**

Exercise:

Notice the next time that you are feeling particularly challenged and pull out your travel pen and paper to record whatever the challenge is that is coming up for you. . . Set the intention to revisit these challenges by re-reading them exactly one week later for an entire month.

At the end of the one month, ask yourself, "What is the recurring theme?" Whether or not you find a recurring theme, take a moment to pause and consider what the opposite of each experience is. Ask, *"What actions might I take to counteract the limiting old story?"* Write three actions you can take on behalf of the new storyline that you are creating: three actions for that **day.** Three actions for that **week.** For that **month.** And, for the **year.** Notice your language choices as your craft your actions **and** refer to *Chapters 19, 20, 21* of *Conquer Trauma Drama: Get Your Life Back* for a comprehensive guide to your choiceful writing and speaking.

Why this is important: Stopping the cycle (of old stories) is key for gaining increased life purpose (and passion) for today and what is to come. Once you have completed writing two or three main story themes in your life that are inherently limiting, highlight the new story's contrasting thoughts. Doggie-ear that page (fold the corner of that page in your journal) or bookmark that page with a small post-it and return to the highlighting portion when you are feeling down or particularly challenged in any given moment.

Your Notes

FOR THIS SHEET, REFERENCE CHAPTER 17

My Pet Store Realization

Fun Fact: As quoted in the book, *Seven: How Many Days of The Week Can Be Extraordinary,* Sir James Jeans, British astronomer, is quoted as saying, *"Thanks to electron microscopes and modern physics we are now beginning to see that the universe more closely resembles one big thought rather than one big machine."* This physicist also said, *"To travel hopefully is better than to arrive."* Meaning, that questions, *and the journey that is the cause for the questions,* are more rewarding to explore, and more life-giving to consider, than the ultimate outcome, no matter what that outcome might be, could ever be.

Questions:

1) Since your most recent trauma have you noticed people interact with you differently? *If so, how?* **Write down your answer.**
2) How do you ultimately want people to interact with you in the wake of a Big-T trauma? **Write down your answer.**
3) How do you perceive yourself differently since your last big life experience? **Write down your answer in 4-6 sentences maximum.**
4) How do you see yourself as being more capable since the event(s)? **Write your answer.**
5) How do you perceive yourself as being less capable since the event(s)? **Write your answer.**
6) What people, things or ideas reinforce both of these assessments of yourself? **Write down your answer.**
7) On any given day, who has the final say on who you are? **Write your answer.** How do you *feel* about that? What do you *think* about that? **Write your answers.**

Exercise:

Step 1: Get together with 1-3 other people. Each of you write down **(3) life-changing events** that have occurred in your life that you are comfortable sharing.

Step 2: Once each person shares their life changing three events the other people in the group write *what they think* might be a byproduct of the speaker having had these experiences. **List one possible but not definite byproduct** for each of the (3) experiences that have been named by the speaker.

Step 3: Once everyone has shared (3) of their life's biggest events **and** once everyone has given the speaker their opinion of possible byproducts it is important that those who have listened **not** comment, reject the ideas presented by the speaker, or vocalize that you agree. *As a listener to other people's ideas, do not agree or disagree. Just listen.* Once you have listened to the opinions of others you may say, "*Thanks for your opinion.*" *It is important that you as a listener to other people's perceived possible byproducts also do not agree or disagree.*

Your Notes

FOR THIS SHEET, REFERENCE CHAPTER 18

You Make the Call

Fun Fact: An article published in *Psychology Today* titled, *Is There Such a Thing as Shame Power,* writes, *"As a preventive measure, shame may work. But once the deed is done, shame is more likely to inspire self-sabotage than self-control."* Therefore, the investing in and holding onto shame in one's life is more a curse than a blessing. People's experiences need to be integrated, with the element of inner (or interpersonal shame) removed from their felt, *and spoken,* thought process. This resolution of replacing shame with self-acceptance and self-love aids in the mastery of the day-to-day process of moving forward and living a fulfilling and rewarding life.

Questions:

1) Think of the first Big-T trauma that comes to your mind that you have experienced in your lifetime thus far. **Write it down now.** During the trauma, did you fight, take flight, or freeze? **Write down your answer.**
2) If you fought, what in your previous life experiences may have impressed upon you that you might win? On the contrary, if you ran, what in your life experiences might have told you that you needed to run? If you froze, upon reflection, what do you think may or may not have contributed to the part of your brain that makes the unconscious choice to freeze? **Write down your reflection in maximum one paragraph (4-6 sentences).**
3) Regardless of what the body's response was in that moment, what were your feelings about the event in the 24-hours that had followed the event? **Write your answer.**
4) What are your feelings today about this particular event? **Write your answer.**
5) What are the beliefs that have evolved about your personhood as a result of the experience? **Write your answer.**
6) How might it be best to change those beliefs moving forward? **Write your answer.**
7) Choose a physical movement that you may like to associate with the victorious feeling of knowing that you *can* create life anew in your here and now. The chosen physical movement can be anything. **Write down what you choose for it to be.**

Note: if you are having a difficult time seeing the bright side of the particular event you have chosen to focus on for this one exercise refer to Chapter 41, How to Neutralize Your Thoughts.

Exercise:

Write affirmations to resemble the new intention of beginning to shift the outdated beliefs associated with this experience. You have outlined the beginnings of your intentions in your answer to number (4). Share with a mentor, or trusted family member or friend to receive feedback on how you might structure the affirmations to best serve you as well as implement them into your day-to-day life beginning today. *If you are in one of Jo Standing's programs do the following:* Write affirmations for your intentions to change the outdated beliefs associated with this experience only. Send them to her via the email you have on file. *They will be evaluated and possibly restructured to best reflect your core desires and intentions and mailed back to you!*

Your Notes

FOR THIS SHEET, REFERENCE CHAPTER 19

Affirmations

Fun Fact: *Big Think,* published an article called *True Meditation is the Science of Observing Your Thoughts.* It is conceived and written by Jon Kabat-Zinn. Kabat-Zinn yields the following valuable insight, "*Thoughts are like the weather of the mind.*" He also says, "*Thoughts are bubbles that are waiting to be popped by awareness.*" Therefore, our thoughts, no matter if we like it or not, are the determining factor of what kind of day we're having, cloudy or sun-filled, and awareness *can* shift our thoughts. However as Gary Douglas, says, our action-packed choices ultimately will shape our awareness. Not the other way around. So, will you choose to think new uplifting thoughts, in order to yield greater awarenesses, happiness and prosperity? It is key to create new thoughts in your prayers, in your journaling, and in your day-to-day conversations . . . *(no matter how silly or awkward it might feel!)*

Questions:

1) How often throughout the day do you observe your thoughts? Would you say ten percent of the time? Fifty percent, or higher? **Write down your answer.**
2) How often, or what percentage of the time, do you hear people you are in conversation with affirm positive uplifting things about themselves or the world? **Write down your answer.**
3) What thought have you had multiple times today or over the course of the last week about something you want to change? **What is it? Write it down.**
4) What fears do you have around taking the necessary action in order to stop having the recurring thought? **Write your answer.**
5) On the contrary, what healthy anticipations beneath the fear might you have around the recurring thought? (Remember, there must be some element of a healthy dynamic or else you wouldn't be obsessing over the particular thought(s). *This goes with the universal fact that where there is dark, there is light, and vice versa.*) **Write down your findings now.**

Exercise:

1) **Exercise #1:** Begin journaling stream of consciousness for ten minutes every morning right when you wake up. Then, for the next week following that week do *not* engage in this practice. At the end of the second week note how you felt in the week of doing this practice compared to the week when you did not. Based on your findings, what would you like to do moving forward? Five minutes? More? Less? In the morning? Afternoon? Evening? Right before you go to bed? **Why?** Make sure you carefully consider all of your answers and write them down. If you have a coach, counsellor, mentor or psychologist make sure to tell them of your new goal, too.
2) **Exercise #2:** Make a list of the next five times you hear people saying something of a positive nature **and** in the moment repeat back to them in an affirming way what they said. For example: You are in the grocery store and someone looks at you and says, "What a relief to see the price of apples dropping, again!" You say, "Yes, it is a relief; I guess I'll be buying more apples this week!" Or, you're in a public bathroom at your favorite restaurant standing at the sinks and the person next to you takes a deep breath and as they look in the mirror congratulates themselves,"*I think I lost my extra weight this winter!*" They look extremely satisfied. You might say, "*That must feel awesome.*" You reinforce the positive.

Your Notes

FOR THIS SHEET, REFERENCE CHAPTER 20

How to Write Affirmations

Fun Fact: In order to accomplish great things we must remove distractions and "need to do" items from the physical space where we plan to execute the task that is believed by us to slowly but surely deliver us to the greatness within ourselves. In the piece titled, *The Science of Peak Human Performance*, TIME magazine talks about what happens when the part of the brain labeled the prefrontal cortex successfully goes quiet. In a possibly more relatable piece, published in TheBioneer.com, the author discusses how it is important to handle any of the things that might distract the mind *first* so that the prefrontal cortex does not get engaged. The prefrontal cortex handles things such as *'personality expression, decision making, and moderating social behaviour,'* as Wikipedia readily describes. Therefore, it is best to reinforce in an affirmation that everything that needs to be taken care of in the given moment has already successfully been taken care of and that you are now free to leave the regular conscious mind and delve into the fruits of the subconscious brain by going into the full 'flow state', beyond the prefrontal cortex operations, as Mihaly Csikszentmihalyi coined in the 1970's.

Questions:

1) **List** (3) things that are unknown in your life at the moment.

2A) In general, what is your relationship to the unknown? On a consistent basis, how do you find yourself regarding the unknown in your life? Is it primarily exciting? Scary? Or? What do you feel about the unknown? **Write your answer.**

2B) If you find yourself getting scared when faced with a 'great unknown,' how long does it usually take you to shift out of fear? **Write your answer.** What preliminary action or thought has helped you to actually move past the state of fear? **Write your answer.** If you do not have a method, yet, brainstorm by writing down (1) or (2) words or actions that you might consider in order to challenge fear the next time it arises within you.

3) On a scale of 1-10 how open are you to success in your personal life? **Write your answer.**

4) On a scale of 1-10 how open are you to success in your professional life? **Write your answer.**

5) What do you do to avoid success in various areas of your life? Are there recurring objections to success when you find yourself presented with the ability for you to be successful in any one

given area? If yes, what are they and what do you want to change about your reaction(s)? **Write your answers.**

Exercise:

Ask a neutral person, someone who isn't overly-invested in your life's specific outcomes but can see your strengths, what they think you have the potential of being successful at in your life. Ask them to name 2-3 things. It might be a career or a pastime or a role in your community that they can see you being great at. *It can be anything.* Follow each thing they give you with one reason you personally think that *might be a possibility.* Also give one reason why you think it will **not** be a possibility. Then, follow the single objection you have named with the words, *". . .and, even though I just said that, I know that deep down anything is possible."*

Your Notes

FOR THIS SHEET, REFERENCE CHAPTER 21

How to Say Affirmations

Fun Fact: In the New York Times, it is read, "Researchers have determined that mirrors can subtly affect human behavior, often in surprisingly positive ways." And, "Subjects tested in a room with a mirror have been found to work harder." If our brain works harder to deliver results when we are knowingly being watched, even if it is by ourselves, then this directly shows the significance of using mirrors in affirmation work in the process of uncovering our best selves. Remember, that by stepping into our best selves we serve much more than individual ourselves, we serve our communities and people we may not even ever meet in person if we think big enough and reach high enough and far enough.

Questions:

1) When do you find it most comfortable to communicate your deepest thoughts with others? **For example:** *When you're out in nature? After you've eaten a big meal? On the telephone? Via email?* Or? **Write your answer and why you think this is.**
2) When do you feel most inclined to reflect on your thoughts or journal? What time of day is it? What part of the house are you in? Or, are you somewhere else outside of where you live? **Write your answer.**
3) What contributes to your well-being in this or these settings? **Write your answer.**
4) What brings you the most confidence in your life? What factors? Which people? Places? Material things? When are you most confident? **Write your answers.**

Exercise:

Go to the settings where you find it the most comfortable to be with your thoughts in order to sit with the affirmations that you have written down in previous pages. Hold a small hand mirror in front of you. Silently lip sync 3-5 affirmations that you have written down. Notice the expression on your face. Now, invite even more expression to appear on your face as you say the 3-5 affirmations again, only this time outloud *and not lip synced.* Take a deep breath through your nose. Now, hold a smile on your face for 5 seconds… the largest smile you can muster. Finally, wrap your arms around yourself in the way that feels best and HUG YOURSELF. (Don't undervalue this step until you try it!)

Your Notes

FOR THIS SHEET, REFERENCE CHAPTER 22

Taking Feelings On Board

Fun Fact: In the Scientific American, a scientist and author, Damasio, recognizes the health factor and gain of acknowledging and intentionally using the mind to balance feelings, or as Damasio says, emotions. The article reads, "He recommends contrasting the negative emotions such as sadness and fear with joy, for example. He understood this kind of practice as a way to reach an inner peace and stoic equanimity." In order to master our feelings or emotions we must first be open to identifying what they are. Damasio and his wife extensively research the complex human in all our wonder as a species. We must be open to developing a heightened sense of both our physical and non-physical selves in order to realize our lives to new levels and enrich our lives to greater degree and reward.

Questions:

1) When are you most willing to use feeling words? **Write your answer.**
2) In what scenarios are you most resistant to using feeling words? **Write your answer.**
3) What environments help you to both feel and express your feelings? Is it a natural setting? Or, otherwise? **Write your answer.**

Exercise:

In the book, *Conquer Trauma Drama: Get Your Life Back,* the following statement is read, "Feelings are to create connection. If you are using them for any other reason then you are creating drama." So, next time you are feeling an adverse emotion such as jealousy, anger, (or the exact opposite a.k.a. indifference) I invite you to assess what the mental thought *pattern* or mental thought form *in that moment* is. Observing our thoughts is not always easy: pause for a moment, take a breath and willfully ask yourself what it is that is bothering you in that moment. What is the cause for the adverse feeling? What are you thinking about in that moment that is further anchoring you in or contributing to your feeling of discontent? Write down all of these answers in your carry around journal with your favorite pen or pencil. Make sure that it is easy to write with your chosen type of pen or pencil so that the words can flow more effortlessly.

Note: The subconscious will spin effortlessly without any conscious interference from your brain power. *Unless. . .you focus! Figure out the cause. And, begin to change the mental thought patterns and inclinations into new ones that serve you* ***TODAY***. This is an ongoing practice that is never perfected. (And, that's the fun part. . . we are a continual work in progress!) We only build upon story, upon story, in our lives, to continue to shape the lives that we most desire in order to continue to stay fulfilled and complete.

Now, practice this exercise with a neutral thought centered around balancing your feeling with your present, *though temporary as all are,* reality. . . For instance, "I feel annoyed; I wish that he might have shared the change of plans with me. . .*and that's okay.*"

Write the feeling first, then what you want to be different. Then, follow with ". . .*and that's okay.*"

So long as we can accept life, life is always going to turn out ok. Acknowledgement of what-is and acceptance of what-is, is the first key to starting to re-shape our reality to create something new. This fact is one of life's many ironies, just as the fact that sometimes we need to go back in order to go forward is, also, an irony.

Your Notes

FOR THIS SHEET, REFERENCE CHAPTER 23

Counteract Victim Talk

Fun Fact: In the highly-regarded publication, The Atlantic, the following is stated, "Any time someone defaults to questioning what a victim could have done differently to prevent a crime, he or she is participating, to some degree, in the culture of victim-blaming." It is absolutely vital to our ability to be able to shift and thrive to acknowledge, or possibly remember, that every human experiences the state of victim at some point or another within the duration of their lives. Oftentimes, more than once and on the various human levels of emotional, mental, spiritual, and physical selves. Compassion for ourselves and others is key to pushing beyond limitation and gathering understanding to new extent.

Questions:

1) When was the last time that you were in a situation when you suddenly felt completely out of control? **Write your answer.** How did you respond in this situation? **Write your answer.** Were you more focused on creating a solution or on the details of the problem? **Write your answer.** At the time of the situation did you most identify with, "*being of a situation,*' instead of 'temporarily *in a situation?' Consider your answer before proceeding to number two.*
2) Name (3) times when you victoriously took action in your life in a challenging or oppressive time. **Write each of the times down in affirmative words that acknowledge your strengths.**
3) What do you think people might say or do if you were to conquer all your challenges right now? Consider the challenges that you know the people in your life are aware of that you have shared with others. **Write what you anticipate them saying and feeling.**
4) Think about and list at least (2) ways that you create healthy space between yourself and others when you are finding the need for it. What do you say to the people you require space from? **Write your answers.**
5) Are there certain activities that you go to for comfort or solace? What are (4)? **Write your answer.**

Exercise:

This exercise is a visualization practice that you may do once or multiple times. So, I suggest that you find a safe and quiet place, a bedroom or any other place that falls into this category is fine. If and when you are feeling victimized by another person's actions or words come to this exercise and visualization technique. Begin, by taking several deep breaths in the lower portion of your belly. Close your eyes with your back elongated and supported with pillows, a yoga mat or a wall.

Envision a life-sized healing quartz crystal to appear in front of you. Keep breathing deeply while actively envisioning the following... The life-sized crystal runs the whole length of your body, from your feet to your head and possibly a little beyond. Keep breathing deeply. Imagine that you may now feel into your body and sense where your personal energy may be stuck or compromised based on your feelings and experience with the individual you have chosen to consider for the purpose of this exercise. Keep breathing and imagine as you do so that you may dispel or discharge this person's energy from your physical body and that as you do so this old, stagnant or unwanted energy is leaving your body. Keep breathing and continue to picture your ability to give unwanted body sensations over to this healing energy crystal where they are then immediately dissolved.

Finally, as a last step, imagine the person who you are experiencing the challenges with to appear on the direct opposite side of the life-sized crystal. As you continue to breathe, and as you are ready, envision this person walking into the crystal that is before you.

Remember, you are looking at the crystal, and are not inside of it.

Once the person has entered the space of the life-sized healing crystal imagine both the crystal and that person are dispersing into a brilliant, sparkling, white light. This can look like small pieces of confetti exploding all over a room. Keep breathing and see that this person, and any harm or discontent you felt connected to this person's thoughts and/or actions, are now free from your space. To complete, invite yourself to imagine a deep rooting from your feet and tailbone into the core of the earth to firmly plant yourself into the here and now and in the present moment. Slowly open your eyes and welcome your physical surroundings to come into view, again. Write stream of consciousness for the next 5-minutes at minimum. Try 10-minutes or more if you can!

Your Notes

FOR THIS SHEET, REFERENCE CHAPTER 24

Why Boundaries Are a Gift

Fun Fact: In the publication PsychCentral it is neatly written, "According to psychologist Katayune Kaeni, PsyD, boundaries are: "knowing your own limits, needs and desires in order to maintain your sense of self and express that to another person, so you can teach them how to treat you." The challenge with many Big-T trauma survivors is that the sense of self is largely eroded when afflicted with PTSD. The sense of self becomes challenging to discern because of the sense of self-knowing being diminished because of the flurry of thought that often accompanies anxiety and the cyclical nature of thought that is often a byproduct of depression and a heightened sense of fear in the mind-body complex and central nervous system. Science shows that with perseverance and kindness to the self all states of mind can be combatted, or managed with great success, including anxiety and depression. Boundaries, too, become more easily navigated with practice and routine attention to how they need to be constructed and communicated.

Questions:

1) What is your definition of boundaries? **Write your answer.**
2) What do they mean to you personally? **Write your answer.**
3) What do they mean to you professionally? **Write your answer.**
4) What feelings come up for you when you hear the word "boundaries"? **Write your answer.**

   Note: For some, we get the sense that we might be oppressed by having "too many boundaries", when actually boundaries are something that are self-created and defined in accordance with what *we each individually require in our lives.* They are best realized when shared as gifts with other people and not as strict guidelines. People receive notification of what our boundaries are more openly and graciously when we speak them as a way to connect more deeply with the people in our lives.
5) The abo acknowledged, after answering the above questions also write down one time when you felt great about sharing your boundaries, and one time when you felt it was an unpleasant experience.

2) Boundaries are best spoken *before* we have too strong of adverse feelings. The best time to announce a boundary is when we notice we feel uncomfortable with a situation, this is the opportune time to access *why*, and then to share what you are hoping to put in place as a *new* way to connect with that individual.

This said, can you think of **feelings and thoughts** that you have when a boundary of yours has been crossed and you have not told *the person about the boundary*? **On the other hand,** if you have told someone about a boundary *and* it is still crossed, what feelings and thoughts are most likely to be there for you? **Write your answer.**

Note: What is the best way to not be victimized over the truth of your boundaries? Speaking our individual truth is the key to not victimizing ourselves in the event of another person acting in ways that we do not agree with. We must place high value on what we have said and done and the *efforts we have made to speak our truth* regardless of how that person thoughtfully responds or unconsciously reacts to our spoken desires and requests.

4) Can you think of any other methods you may have used or may use in the future to overcome the disappointment or anger that you may have in relation to another's actions, *even though you have been clear with your desire to connect in a way that honors both of you,* and the other person (or people) involved have not listened to your spoken boundary? **Please write your possible future actions or chosen thoughts here that you think may be helpful to you to shift out of victim mode.**
5) Define what personal freedom is to you. **Write your answer.**
6) Based off of the different types of boundaries listed in *Conquer Trauma Drama: Get Your Life Back,* which defined boundary do you find most informative? **Write your answer.** Were you aware of all of the types of boundaries listed in *Chapter 24*? **Write your answer.** If not, write down what you might do to learn more about the particular type of boundary that is new to you...

Exercise:

Ask a friend about these same questions. Intend to listen closely so that you may also learn about how other people may or may not respond to the above possibilities. Make sure to listen closely, with non-judgment and curiosity. Neutral listening is best. Do not validate them with praise or try and disprove what they have to say... Remember, this is *their* experience.

Your Notes

FOR THIS SHEET, REFERENCE CHAPTER 25

How to Break Through Denial

Fun Fact: Fun Fact: Salman Rushdie, said, "History is always an ambiguous affair. Facts are hard to establish, and capable of being given many meanings. Reality is built on our own prejudices, gullibility, and ignorance, as well as on knowledge and analysis." Based on the author's understanding of reality we can further see that reality is constantly sifting and changing based on a person's lens, or on a society's latest understanding(s). Therefore, we must increase our own personal sensitivity to both the facts and experiences that are the foundation from which we operate our own lives from on a daily basis. We need to be curious in order to withstand our own false biases and misperceptions about the occurrences within our lives so that we may know our own truths. And, realize more fully what is is that we want our lives to look like on a continual basis.

Questions:

1) Name (3) aspects of your life that you are not yet fully content with as of today. Write them down.
2) List (3) things in your life that you are not yet fully content with as of today. Write them down.
3) Write (3) reoccurring thoughts you had today that you are not fully **content** with as of today. List them here. Follow with (1) reason for each item that you are not satisfied with the thought.
4) In the English dictionary, a "victor" is a person who defeats an enemy or opponent in a battle, game, or other competition. . . In the classic sense, a victor means a "winner", "champion", or "conqueror". *Define what it means to you to be a victor in your life. Include mentally, physically, emotionally and possibly spiritually, too.*

Exercise:

List (3) **ways** that you have struggled as a result of your most traumas and **(6) ways** that you have grown, *and are growing*, because of the occurrence of that traumatic event in your life.

Next, journal at least one paragraph (4-5 sentences) about self-judgments that came up as a byproduct of the traumas in your life. Now, **list 2-3 ways you** may start to disprove those previous judgments about yourself **today** and in the days to come.

Note: You may find creative ways to challenge old judgments about yourself through small actions, thoughts, or conversations that you choose to engage in with others.

Your Notes

FOR THIS SHEET, REFERENCE CHAPTER 26

Develop Your Feeling Detector

Fun Fact: Many people see feelings as weak or a source of embarrassment. Also, some think that having, nurturing, or sharing, feelings makes you vulnerable to an irreversible negativity either from the outside or inside. Really, feelings that are held inside become more dangerous to the person than any outcome that may occur as a byproduct of expressing them. One needn't express feelings immediately upon feeling them, or to go directly to the source of the cause for the feelings in order to be effective in managing the inward dynamic experience caused by the feelings. The mind can be just as much attached to the fear of sharing feelings as it is to keeping the feelings alive and well and making them the centerpiece of your life. Getting the mind attentively engage with managing feelings is crucial to accelerating healing and life empowerment within an individual in order to continue to expand and prosper in relationships. In an article by BBC, scientist say that the challenge of putting emotion into words is due to a breakdown in communication between the hemispheres.

Questions:

1) What is the felt process of happy for you? What does it feel like in your body? **Write your answer down.**
2) What are (1) or (2) thoughts that usually accompany the state of happy for you? **Write your response down once fully considered.**
3) Repeat (1) and (2) in relationship to the following states of being: sadness, joy, anger, lonely, helpless, nervous, anxious, depressed, tired. If you do not experience one or more of these do not write down a reply for that. Or, if you want to explore another state of feeling that is not listed here please do so following the guidance of the questions in number (1) and (2). **Begin your exploration now.**
4) Closely examine what your triggers usually are **both internally** (your own thoughts/perceptions/beliefs) **and *externally*** (for example, someone sitting in "your" chair/calling you a derogatory name, giving you flowers or a compliment, etc.) for each of the feeling states you've examined in the above. **Note:** triggers can be both negative and positive. So, include an answer for what often can trigger joy or happiness, too, such as kind actions. **Write your answers.**

Exercise:

The next time you are in an argument with someone, or a simple disagreement on whatever level of intensity, and this is someone with whom you have an overall amicable relationship with, ask them to participate in the following exercise with you:

Inquire of and write down what the other person's top 3-5 thoughts are *and* their top 3-5 feelings are concerning the disagreement. The friend or loved one is participating by giving you their top 3-5 thoughts and feelings. Get clear and write them down *exactly* as they are spoken.

Now, ask your friend or loved one to do the same for you. Request that they now write down exactly what you say in regards to what *your* top 3-5 thoughts and feelings concerning the disharmony at hand.

Next, both of you hold the piece of paper with the other person's thoughts and feelings written on them and once you have decided who will go first, read the other person's outloud. Lend as much neutrality and compassion to the other person's perspective and feelings as possible in your tone and body language.

Once both of you have completed doing so begin to write down how the experience of doing so felt for you. Now, exchange the pieces of paper and read one another's answers either silently or aloud. Consider meditating for 3-5 minutes in silence before talking about anything else.

Your Notes

FOR THIS SHEET, REFERENCE CHAPTER 27

Practice Moderation

Fun Fact: Science will tell you that thoughts come from a firing of the brain's infrastructure in response to either the previous thought, a long stored memory, or some external stimuli. Spirituality might tell you that it is a byproduct of sensing of energy around you, the soul's desire being stoked, or even the remembering of a past lifetime. Or, as Forbes writer and neuroscientist, Yohan John, also writes, "The neuronal patterns that mediate and enable thought and behavior have *proximal* and *distal* causes." Thought is a mystery but what is certain is that with the continued evidence and listening in on our own thoughts, we can change our lives one brain spark at a time!

Questions:

1) For the next exploration, consider that *feeling* is different from *thinking*. Also, consider that moderation means living our day to day lives in balance, especially in consideration of both the influx and outpour of our personal time and energy, and the basis of how it is used. That said, in what life areas do you *feel* you are most balanced? In what areas do you *think* you are most balanced? **Write your answer.**
2) In the reverse, in what areas might you *feel* the most unbalanced? In what areas do you *think* you might be unbalanced? **Write your answers.**
3) For the next exploration, consider that *wanting* is different from *needing*. Make a list of (5) "things" you currently **want** in your life. It can be a relationship, a feeling, a material good, or a travel experience, among many other "things". **Then, write for "why" after each answer.**
4) Next, write (5) things you absolutely need in your life right now. **Follow each answer with your "why".**
5) **Write (5) things** you've thought about today. Write down your answer now. Which ones do you want to think more about out of the ones you've now listed? Write your answers now and follow each one with your "why".
6) Write (5) things you've felt today. **Write your answer now.** Which ones do you want to feel more of out of the things that you've listed? **Write your answers down.** Follow each answer with your "why" to reinforce why you've given this answer.

7) Next, what is (1) action step you might take to introduce more of both of these states of being and narratives into your life? **Write your answer.**

Exercise:

Discuss with a trusted confidante how confusing what you *want* and what you *need* in the past has created drama, confusion, a sense of discontentment, or suffering. Please note: Make sure to bring your intimate sharing back to the fact that you have now successfully realized these findings. And, in that realization, there is a divine sense of power and ability to move forward to create new experiences based on the feelings you now choose, and the thoughts you're now cultivating. **Write down at least (1) realization you have had as a byproduct of your discussion and inward exploration. *Note:** Chapter 28 of *Conquer Trauma Drama: Get Your Life Back* does not have a correlated worksheet found in this book because the chapter within the paperback is already set up as questions and exercises. Please proceed to Chapter 29 of the Breakthrough Curriculum on the next page after your notes page.

Your Notes

FOR THIS SHEET, REFERENCE CHAPTER 29

The Best Question for Helpers to Ask

Fun Fact: Brene Brown Ph.D., a hero to many, illustrates the negative lasting power of shame in her TED speaking and writing. An example of the unveiling of her work is in this statement, "Shame corrodes the very part of us that believes we are capable of change." Shame, beyond the gift of realization that we must lead ourselves to change, is a hindrance to our growth and the very accomplishment of the life that we know deep down we want to live. We must therefore reach beyond the weight of the initial shame of false action and temper ourselves to learn to react with greater internal response, and less outward knee-jerking compulsion. With gentleness toward ourselves, in times where we are yielded this luxury, we have the potential of expanding far wider and realizing our potential with far greater vastness and attainment of inner wealth. We have the ability to grow to new measures and seek the best within ourselves.

Questions:

1) **List** a time when you felt happy about the impact you had on either a friend or a stranger who you sensed was in need of love, attention, or some other support. **Write your answer as well as why you chose to contribute to that person's life.**
2) Conversely, **list** a time when you felt remorseful or sad because of something you had said or done that seemed to make a situation unpleasant. **Write your answer.**
3) What *positive, neutral or negative* judgments did you carry away from that experience? **Write your answer.** List the judgments about yourself first then any judgements about the world in general that you may have developed because of the experience.

Special Note: A **positive judgment** is judging a situation, person or thing in a way that puts the person, thing or situation at an advantage. For example: you judge that the senior at the market, although they are elderly, is strong and capable of pushing the full cart. A **neutral judgment** is an unarguable truth. So, say that you see that same elder and you simply notice that that person is older than you. A **negative judgment** puts that same person, place or thing at a disadvantage in the event that the person or people on the receiving end of the judgment were to believe in the spoken judgment. For example, you see that same elderly person pushing the cart and vibe them by thinking, "That person is so old! *Ugh! Yuck!* I hope I never get *that old!* Or, "They're so old that they should be paying someone to grocery shop for them!" As a general rule, negative judgments demean a person, place or thing.

4) Think of a time when you wanted to help someone but did not choose to do so. **Write down that experience and include why you decided not to help them.** Now, think of one pro that may have come about in your life as a byproduct of **not** helping them. **Write that down in positive life-affirming words.**
5) **Write** down (1) *person* you want to be of support to in your today.
6) What are (3) of the bravest things you have ever done in your life? **Write and then speak out loud the first (3) that come to mind first without filtering yourself or your answers.** Notice any judgments that might come up as you contemplate this, about yourself, or your life, whether they are positive, neutral or negative. Just be of aware of them **if** they surface rather than developing too much of a story about them.
7) **Write** what you felt during each of the (3) brave moments you recollected in the past number and follow it with, "... and I am open and willing to feel that way, again."

Exercise:

Look at your answer to number two as to why you may not have helped someone in some fashion or another when they needed the help of someone. Contemplate if your resistance had anything to do with the fear of the unknown. Write yes or no. Next, think about the last (2) times that you were faced with the unknown in various areas of your life. What was either your knee jerk reaction or cultivated response to the unknown? Write your answers. Now, put on your "Hero Suit" and look at your life experiences that you've listed again. What might be an alternative response to each of these (5) experiences? Imagine and write about each alternative response and note how you feel after "mentally living" aka imagining each alternative. **Begin writing now.**

Your Notes

FOR THIS SHEET, REFERENCE CHAPTER 30 & 31

What's in a Yes for You?

Fun Fact: The New York Magazine notes that NYU psychologist Gabriele Oettingen developed WOOP, a four-step process for achieving a challenging goal in which the letters stand for Wish, Outcome, Obstacles, Plan. The attainment of any vision is reliant on many factors and there are sky high debates as to whether or not picturing your life as you want it actually works or not. The best way to know is picking yourself up by the bootstraps and giving it a try! For the duration of this worksheet you are encouraged to believe that anything is possible! Afterall, no one ever accomplished anything thinking, feeling, or strongly believing that their aim was a worthless effort.

Questions:

1) **List** (5) things you see yourself definitely say yes to if or when the opportunity presents itself. **Write your answer.**
2) Now, **list** the answers in number one in order of priority relevance; which one do you really want to happen the most? **Write your answer.**
3) **List** who in your life might be most supportive if you were to accomplish or receive the blessings or advancements listed in number one. Whether you do or do not have an answer to this as of right now list, next the character traits of the people you want around to celebrate your successes with you. **Write your answer.**
4) When does your mind feel the most focused? In what situations? Environments? **Write down your answers now.**
5) When does your body feel the most ease of movement? When you're swimming? Gardening? When you're playing with your kids or grandkids? **List your answer(s) now on paper. Feel free to list up to (10) maximum.**
6) Has anyone ever told you that you have 'great energy'? Or, have you ever told anyone that? What do you think is meant by that statement? Write your answer. What do you think gives someone 'great energy'? **Write your answer.**

Exercise:

In Chapter Thirty-One of ***Conquer Trauma Drama: Get Your Life Back*** we learn about electromagnetic fields factor into the likelihood of our personal resilience. That said, let's begin by practicing a physical and mental exercise that strengthens our human electromagnetic field. First, think of a detrimental or antagonizing thought that you might have had about yourself or your life in the recent past. And, possibly a cycle that is related to that thought and consequently shows up in your life because of that particular thought that you want to get rid of.

Write it down in an affirmative statement, "I am freeing myself of this/these thought(s) (__*state the thought*___).

Next, sit down with arms length of space all around your body. Reach your arms out to either side and make sure you have lots of space. First whisper, and then speak aloud the new thought and/or cycle you last wrote that has either temporarily or permanently replaced the old thought or cycle.

Inhale as you reach your arms out to the sides with palms up as you imagine bringing the new life dynamic you've mentioned and named into your life in all areas. Exhale as you place palms facing down and arms now moving down from the up position that they were just in.

Imagine you are exhaling the outdated thoughts and cycles out of your body, mind and present experience as you picture returning each of these old thoughts, or ways of being, down to the depth of the earth with the power and strength of your mind to where they can then be transformed into all that nurtures you and your loved ones just as the earth does.

Sit quietly for a minimum of 60-seconds with eyes open or closed. Finally, wrote stream of consciousness for 2-3 minutes about how that experience was for you. Keep your words as positively geared toward life-giving thoughts as possible.

Your Notes

FOR THIS SHEET, REFERENCE CHAPTER 32

How to Embrace Your Body's Experience

Fun Fact: In an article by Scientific American, Christopher Del Negro, a neurophysiologist at the College of William & Mary says, "Breathing is about staying alive on one level, but it's also connected to emotional life." This quote is a brilliantly simple encapsulation of the ability to possibly control our personal emotional state by mental force. When we breathe in a controlled fashion we can moderate the extent of our reactions or even thoughtfully disengage from reacting at all. Remember that all bodily experiences are just that... *experiences.* And, they are signposts that we may explore so that we may then best master the outcome of our lives. One breath and step at a time.

Questions:

1) For this step, identify a trauma you want to further clear from your present experience and how it is affecting your life. **Write it down.** Next, set a timer to (1) minute so that when it rings it acts as a reminder to return to the room and present space around you in the now. Please Note: Before you start the timer *set the intention* that once the timer starts you will be exploring what physical sensations are retriggered in your body when you think about the past event that you have identified wanting to restructure your relationship to in the present moment. **Picture in your mind and write down** what it feels like have discovered and remained calm during the process of your self-exploration discovery.
2) **Start the timer.** Let it run for 60-seconds as you focus on the event's effect on your body that you have listed in number (1). Open your eyes now that you have completed the 60-seconds. *If it helps, record yourself speaking this worksheet for a more free-flowing experience as you may then listen to the instructions on playback.* Now that you are aware of what physical responses are triggered in connection to the event, **write down** what you observed in those 60-seconds. **Write your answer(s).**
3) **In writing,** ask yourself what physical movements in day-to-day life activities can positively engage those same specific muscle groups, or general body areas, that you noticed had an unpleasant feel during the 60-seconds of observation. Write, "What might I do to positively engage these areas?"

Then, pause for a moment before writing your answer. You may use your dominant hand and/or non-dominant hand as you **explore these answers.**

For example: if you noticed that your calf muscles tightened up in your exploration of number one then you will list bicycling as a healthy and conscious reinforcement of the engagement of those muscles in a newly life-giving way to reconnect to those muscles.

4) Before taking physical action on number two, **note in writing (1) way** you may foster a sense of letting go in those same muscles you've listed an assertive and healthy way to engage.

For example: for any part of the body that you can reach and apply this to, self-massage is going to be helpful in facilitating a sense of space and freedom in that part(s) of the body that you listed and focused on in one and two. Slow thoughtful walking on grass, soil or sand is also going to massage many areas of the body to bring relief to them. Swimming is another way. List at least (1) way that you may foster a sense of deep calm in that area of the body.

Exercise:

As you complete the physical motion, be sure to take time to **write 2-3 affirmative sentences** that reinforce the newly felt mental, physical and emotional sensations that are present after your practice of your chosen body engagement. If you don't know exactly how to put into words the difference between now and before you practiced this exercise then I invite you to meditate for (5) minutes by stepping away from this exercise and intending to focus single-pointedly on something (it can be anything, gardening, journaling, cooking, talking to a nearby friend.)

Then, return to the intention of clarifying the growth that is possible by coming fully into the changes that this section encourages.

Finally, place the sheet of paper with your specially designed affirmations somewhere that you can see and read it every day for one month after practicing the healthy physical movement you have assigned yourself for (1-5) every day alongside its affirmations.

Note: This is not easy work. So, be gentle with yourself and make sure to call on your support network as you experience each of the powerful effects due in part to the awareness building you are accomplishing by following these steps.

Your Notes

FOR THIS SHEET, REFERENCE CHAPTER 33

How to Use Language as Your Liberator

Fun Fact: Japanese author and researcher, Masaru Emoto, in his studies found that words impact the visible molecular structure of water. This realization is still being learned today by countless people around the world. Considering that up to 60% of the human body is composed of water and the brain and heart are said to be composed of 73% of water this guides one to, at the very least, consider the words and the meaning they carry with great care before using them. In order to activate, and preserve, our health we need not only drink water but also pay close attention to the infrastructure of our daily personal language so that we may engineer our lives to satisfying means. This includes both the language that is used as internal dialogue, quietly to oneself, and the words that are spoken to other people. Enjoy moving forward to your next worksheet!

Questions:

1) **Intentionally write a sentence** down that limits "you" in some way, shape or form. Note: This sentence can be limiting of you specifically, or limiting of "the royal you," meaning a sentence that is limiting, in general, for anyone who might read it. **Begin writing now.**
2) Take the same sentence in number (1) and literally reverse it so that you are now liberated from the previously limiting statement. **Write your reverse sentence now.**
3) **Write (1)** thing, place or person you have denied yourself the experience of, in the course of your life, due to fear. Define what needs to happen in order to give yourself that experience, thing, or chance at that possible relationship. Make sure to speak in an affirmative tone that is life-giving and not life-limiting. **Begin to write your answer.**

Please note: If you still are struggling with the finding or creation of your affirmations, or if you just want a fresh perspective to help you craft new ones, make sure to set up an appointment time with Jo Standing, or one of the other coaches at the Trauma Drama Coaching Institute or Mibo School of Yoga.

Exercise: Ask (5) people you know well enough what they think you are capable of at your best. Make sure to write down the "nuggets of gold" they are giving you about your potential. If you are dissatisfied with what you have heard or cannot find anything uplifting about their answers, then ask (5) more people. Ask as many people as you need until you personally connect with (5) of the answers given to you. Write the feedback that you think to be possible down, *even if you never plan to make a life plan or full commitment of their suggestions!*

Next, choose your favorite of the (5) that you have notated from people's answers.

Now, think of (1) action you can take this week to be one more step toward having the experience you have chosen as being a possibility for you.

Just (1) step and you never have to pursue any further steps if you do not wish to however this is an experience in openness, flexibility and courage. Again, you are just taking (1) step. ***Finally,*** *take the (1) step that you have chosen and journal about how you felt about doing it after you have fulfilled the step!*

***Note: Chapter 34 of *Conquer Trauma Drama: Get Your Life Back* does not have a correlated worksheet in the Breakthrough Curriculum because the chapter within the paperback is already set up as questions and exercises. Please proceed to Chapter 35 next.**

Your Notes

REFERENCE CHAPTER 35

How to Get the Universe to Yield to You

Fun Fact: Jim Sniechowski, Ph.D. and Judith Sherven, Ph.D. write in The Huffington Post about the five markers of knowing you have achieved success with the reference to emotions that you might feel. The anticipated states are, ease, patience, trust and compassion, *both within yourself and between yourself and others,* as well as the individual experience of satisfaction. Since, like Einstein said, there is no such thing as time and space, it is suggested in this book that we sometimes imagine the feelings we want to have first, by tapping into the right brain, so that the left brain then goes into full action mode to make sure there is due reason in one's individual reality for those feelings having been felt in the first place. Emotions move us to take action regardless if we want that to be so or not. To conclude, the Atlantic wrote a piece that discusses why 70 billion is spent in TV advertising in the United States alone. They write, "Successful advertising rarely succeeds through argument or calls to action. Instead, it creates positive memories and feelings that influence our behavior over time to encourage us to buy something at a later date." If we are allowing advertising to drive us to action through the use of feeling then we might as well use that same feeling and emotion to benefit us in our personal and professional lives, *created by ourselves,* too!

Questions:

1) List (1) person who has recently, *or is presently,* challenging your patience. **Write their name down.** Next, **record your voice** in your smartphone or in a free recording system online from your computer as you say the following, *"Even though I am incredibly challenged by this person's actions I now allow myself to imagine her or him as a joyful being existing in happiness with their loved ones outside of this unpleasant circumstance that I have temporarily come to know them in."*
2) Think about your favorite place to visit. **Close your eyes** and imagine you are there for (1) whole minute. **Set a timer** to ensure you come back to the room afterward. Now, listen to your voice recording 3-5 times as you now listen to yourself speaking the words as you silently say and feel the words, too. Note: if you do not have a smartphone, recorder, or computer with you at the moment, just say the statement out loud or quietly to yourself 3-5 more times as you focus intently on the meaning behind the words.

3) **Note: this step requires either a playback device or the support of a friend.** Sit down in a comfortable position and close your eyes halfway or fully. **Take a deep breath.** Make sure to inhale through the nose and exhale through the nose or mouth. **Keep breathing at a slightly slower rate than you usually might.** Now, listen to the recorded affirmation from number one and two as you hold the device up to your **left** ear. This will in turn communicate to your emotional and empathetic right brain in order to activate your whole brain participation in freeing yourself of the toxic or negative response that you are having in response to the person of focus. A friend can say the affirmation in your left ear if you do not have a recording device.
4) Once you have completed number three pause for one minute and **write** down any thoughts that come to mind. If there are any negative judgments then **write** a follow up sentence that either neutralizes or turns the thought into being life-giving.
5) **Consider** what you might offer this individual that you listed in number one as a peace offering, whether it is a measurable action or a thought prayer comprised of 1-3 kind and loving thoughts. **Write your answer down** and imagine sending them that loving gesture or thought prayer. **Take three long breaths** in through your nose and out through your mouth to complete this step.
6) *If possible, a*ctually send them the peace offering that you've constructed in words, or otherwise. This step is optional.

Exercise:

Next, apply the thought prayer or action that you have written in number five *TO YOURSELF*; give yourself the gift of this thought prayer or action. Meaning, how can you convert the idea you had written down for the other person into a loving statement or action for yourself? You may also turn number one into a loving gesture for yourself by saying and/or longhand writing, *"Even though I am challenged right now by some of my own thoughts and actions, I allow myself to live joyfully and in happiness and to exist outside of this unpleasant circumstance with unconditional love and kindness to myself."*

Your Notes

REFERENCE CHAPTER 36

How to Begin Shifting Your Unconscious Mind Patterns

Fun Fact: In music, anticipation is described as the introduction in a composition of part of a chord that is about to follow in full. The state of anticipation can be like that. You know deep in the very core of your being that something great is on the horizon. Expectation is the knowing based on outside information, it's because of what someone or something else has told you. It leaves the outcome of a situation based on someone else's actions and is therefore less empowering. In the dictionary, the archaic first meaning of the word *expectation* was literally defined as, "one's prospects of inheritance." So, this is a great example of placing the power outside of ourselves. With anticipation, we are using our own inner drive to create the circumstances we want from our own resources.

Questions:

1) In your mind and life, what is the difference between anticipation and expectation? Write your answer.
2) From your experience, what are the usual outcomes of when you anticipate something in your professional life? **Write your answer.** What are the usual outcomes when you anticipate something in your personal life? **Write your answer. Make sure to list at least (1) pro and (1) con.**
3) From your experience, what are the usual outcomes of when you expect something in your professional life? **Write your answer.** What are the usual outcomes when you expect something in your personal life? **Write your answer. Make sure to list at least (1) pro and (1) con.**

Please note before proceeding to number four: In order to answer how each one of these feels in your body simply think of the last time you experienced each state of being. Make sure to set a timer at 60-seconds for each focused experience as you allow yourself to visit each one of the following states. Before you begin, choose a physical movement you can do at the sound of the timer. For instance, decide that you will clap or take a deep breath in from your nose, and out through your mouth, at the sound of the timer. This is done in order to ensure you stay connected to the present moment as well as reduce, *if* *not completely remove,* the possibility of slipping too far into your past association with any one feeling. **Continue reading.**

4) When you feel anxiety *where* is it felt in your body? **Write your answer.**
5) When you are anticipating something where is it felt in your body? **Write your answer.**
6) When you are excited about something where is it felt in your body? **Write your answer.**
7) When you are scared or fearful about something where is it felt in your body? **Write your answer.**
8) What is (1) authentic thought you've never thought before that you can create and write down that is centered around your experience of happiness in your life? Use your brain power to come up with (1) new, fresh, thought and then use your mind to grow three supportive details. *Note:* The mind is always running stories, and often mindlessly, and/or cyclically. So, use the brain first to create a new, otherwise unknown-to-you, thought and then let the mind do its job to create a story around the new information you are presenting to it. *You are literally opening up a new portal of possibility when you hold your focus in one area!*

Exercise:

Make an intention log: for the next week when you feel yourself drawn to something or someone do not go to it right away, whether it be food or relationship. Not only will this exercise help you be a powerful creator because you are learning to build your personal energy, you are also building great self-discipline to make it easier for you to achieve your goals as you go along. Once resisting, ask, *"Why am I drawn to this person or thing right now?"* **Write down your answer** in as few words as possible.

Your Notes

FOR THIS SHEET, REFERENCE CHAPTER 37

How to Shift from Chronic Over-Explainer Mode

Fun Fact: The Online Etymology Dictionary quotes Stendhal, author of On Love, in 1822, as saying, " . . . power is the greatest of all pleasures. It seems to me that only love can beat it, and love is a happy illness . . ." Everyone has their own idea of love and power as well as their own relationship to them. In this sheet, begin to explore what your interpretation is based on your own life experience.

Questions:

1) Where do you get your personal sense of power from? **Write your answer.**
2) What is power to you, in an outward sense, in relation to the world? **Write your answer.**
3) Who do you enjoy talking to most in your life right now? **Write your answer.** Why? **Write your answer.** As you think of why you enjoy speaking to this person/people the most . . . how do you feel? **Write your answer.**
4) Where are 2-3 of your most favorite places to go? **Write your answer.**
5) What is one of your favorite songs right now? **Write your answer.**
6) What is one of your most favorite inspiring quotes? **Write your answer.**

Exercise:

Do the following exercise with either a friend, a family member, or with a support group: Share your answers to the above questions with (1) or more people. Instruct them to ask you, "Why do you like that?", "Why do you choose that?", "Why do you feel like that?" Your only answer can be. "Because I do." After they've questioned each one of your choices thank them for their support, smile, and move onto something else in topic of activity.

Note: Chapter 38 and 39 are an entire exercise in and of themselves so the next chapter will read Chapter 40.

Your Notes

FOR THIS SHEET, REFERENCE CHAPTER 40

How to Shift from Victim to Victor

Fun Fact:

Questions:

1) Hypothetically speaking, if you had you NOT experienced your life's most intense traumas, what life experiences might you have missed out on? **Write your answer.**
2) Hypothetically speaking, if you had you NOT experienced your life's most intense traumas, what relationships might you have missed out on? **Write your answer.**
3) Looking at how you might have been unprepared to experience your trauma, what might you do *in the now* physically, mentally, emotionally and/or spiritually to be prepared in the face of such circumstances ever happening again? **Write your answer.**
4) Fill in the blank, *"Part of my truth is that I will always be a victim of ______________, a survivor of ____________, and a resolute thriver after _____________."* In the blank list one true experience you have lived through, that you also acknowledge surviving, and plan on thriving after the fact. The same experience is listed in all three spaces. For an example, refer to the first paragraph of chapter forty in *Conquer Trauma Drama: Get Your Life Back.*
5) In what way might you look at the above experience to allow you to thrive and love in new ways in your life as early as this year? **Write your answer.** This month? **Write your answer.** This week? **Write your answer.** Today? **Write your answer.**
6) On a scale of 1-10 how "meant to be" do you think having the experience you listed in number one was for you and your evolution? (10) being the most meant to be and (1) being the least meant to be. If you rated (5) or above on the "meant to be" scale, write a list of the beneficial outcome(s) you have experienced as a direct result of the event. If you rate (4) or lower write a list of what you are learning from the experience regardless of whether or not you see the experience as having been beneficial. **Begin writing now.**

Exercise:

Have a discussion with a friend, alliance or group member about the difference between action and reaction. Or, do this exercise independently in writing. First, think of and then write down the major stages of your life up until this point. For instance, you might see a life stage as being when you were a child, to when you were an adolescent, to adult to parent to senior. **However, for this exercise, consider your biggest life events and how the occurence of them were grounds for new stages in your life. Go deep** in your exploration on this topic and consider thoughtfully.

How did you manage to mobilize and shift into a new stage of your life? Write your answer.

Think about how conscious thoughts and actions help you shift *from one state of mind* to another. **Write an example of a thought that encourages you to shift on a regular basis.** What do you tell yourself in your own mind to keep going? **Write your answer.**

Your Notes

FOR THIS SHEET, REFERENCE CHAPTER 41

How to Neutralize Your Thoughts

Fun Fact: In a fascinating full-length article (quoted in the Resource portion of this book) The U.S. National Library of Medicine National Institutes of Health published the following statement, "Engagement with creative activities has the potential to contribute toward reducing stress and depression and can serve as a vehicle for alleviating the burden of chronic disease." The next exercise is helping our left and right brains to connect. The hemispheres when equally engaged ignite a certain super power within the individual that would not otherwise be accessed. So, let's use our logic to get creative and our creativity to pinpoint what we most logically need to focus on! Let's get started!

Questions:

1) To begin, think of (1) negative thought. **Write it down.**
2) Think of (1) positive thought that is a direct opposite to the initially negative thought that was intentionally conceived. **Write it down.**
3) **Now, create a neutral thought** also known as a *springboard thought* that will allow you to leap out of the negative end of the "pool of thoughts" and move towards creating the life-giving positive thoughts.

Note: As a very basic example start with the negative thought, "They are horrible people." Now, notice the contrast in thought, "They are excellent people." Observe the *springboard thought* that follows, "Even though I may perceive them as people I may never understand, I acknowledge that in order to be happy I must shift my thoughts." Or, "I can focus on an act of self-love to raise my vibration which in turn helps everyone around me. When I am joyful, it more allows other people to be joyful." *A springboard thought doesn't necessarily take you from one extreme to another extreme in thought process It doesn't request of you to be "fake", or "unrealistic", or not be something you are not. It just invites you to be open. It allows thoughts to shift from life-limiting to life-giving.* One needn't be a raging optimist to practice springboard *thoughts.* Just flexible in mind.

4) **List** the last time you were upset or angry. Write it down in one sentence. Now, see if you can trace what really upset you underneath or below what you originally thought affected you.

Read pages 229, and 230 of *Conquer Trauma Drama: Get Your Life Back* to understand an example that demonstrates that what we are initially upset about is not what we are upset about at all. Shine your light of awareness on what is upsetting at its core and notice the healing power of the awareness all on its own. Awareness is very healing. Write down what you believe was the core trigger aka the deeper reason you were upset outside of the initial surface details or action that took place.

3) Who is someone you can tell about the situation? Before you tell them, **write down exactly what you want to say in order to best articulate your experience of A) being triggered B) realizing it had a root in an experience you had earlier in life.** If you are taking classes with Our Vet Community, the Trauma Drama Coaching Institute, Mibo School of Yoga or The Viva Standing Foundation then take this opportunity to share this realization with a group member. Otherwise, tell a friend, mentor, counselor, or coach. Describe the initial core event or core trigger in the following terms:

- As a narrative without favoring one or more of the characters in the story.
- Remove all judgements or assumptions of other characters' intentions or perceived ulterior motives.
- Emphasize what you said or felt or did. When speaking about others only list their exact actions or words.

Exercise:

Bring this story of recollected events to friends and/or a group support network that you are working with for therapeutic purposes. Ask people, who were not actually in the story in real life, to first hear and/or read the story you have constructed of actions and actual spoken words and ask the other participants to insert in dialogue how the other characters may have felt. Take (5) minutes to journal about this experience once you have completed it. Remember, allow yourself to write first things that come to mind. Do not over think when you are writing stream of consciousness.

Your Notes

REFERENCE CHAPTER 42

How to Master Your Triggers

Fun Fact: Have you ever heard the saying, "Old habits die hard." Or, "Its difficult to teach an old dog new tricks?" Even when we consciously want to change something in our lives, or in this case we figure out how to change a trigger so that it no longer negatively impacts us, there is a grieving period. The truth is we grieve things and people that are not even good for us. Why? Because there is massive comfort in what we have come to know best in our lives right now. The Atlantic says that, "Grief has also been found to aggravate physical pain, increase blood pressure and blood clots, and exacerbate appetite loss." So, when we are grieving a loss, even of something that clearly did not serve us, it is crucial to develop a new habit that reinforces health and well-being to replace the old habit, or way of reacting, to a trigger. Let's move onto questions!

Questions:

1) **Name** the full list of emotions you feel when you are triggered. **Write the list** of emotions down. Acknowledge them *without wanting to change, stifle, or repress them.*
2) **Write the following:**
   - Even though I feel __________ (list the most highly-charged, relevant, feeling experienced when you feel most triggered) I realize I am more than this singular feeling or emotion alone.
3) **Next write the following:**
   - Even though I feel (list the feeling from number two) ____________ when I ____________ I realize that I also exist outside of this singular experience. I realize that my awareness is all powerful.
   - I realize that because I am able to observe (list the feeling from number two) ________________ within myself that this state of mind and being is only *a part* of both my whole experience and existence and a part of myself.
   - I am far more than ________________. (Again list the feeling from number two.)
2) For (5) minutes write stream of consciousness the answer to this question, What are the power of triggers to me? Note: Although the initial thought may be life-limiting, remember to rephrase

the thought in a life-giving way. For example: the initial thought might be something like the following, "Sometimes I get so triggered by my Aunt May telling me that I need a new wardrobe that I want to drain out the sound of her voice by screaming at her." The happiness-granting thought in this instance might be, "I hear the words *'Go buy a new wardrobe,'* from my Aunt May often. I feel completely annoyed and even angry when I hear that. So, instead I choose to remember why I have the wardrobe I have and why I enjoy wearing it so much. I can then easily smile at her because I am undeterred in my way of being and almost even appreciate her words because the end result is I am only brought closer to my whole and complete self! The true self I know as me!" **Begin journaling now.**

3) What are the judgments you hold about yourself for reacting to triggers the way you have done or currently do? **Write them down.**
4) Now, rephrase the judgments as such, "I acknowledge my judgments about myself as blessings that through observation and further examination bring me to the light of my true self. Even my judging self is a part of life's whole beauty in it's entirety as the dark does lead to the light. Therefore, with this knowledge, each time I catch myself judging *or judging myself for judging*, my inclination to do so is diminished. I now allow myself to see, observe and feel the power of shining the light of awareness on my judgments and therefore realize that I am the only person **I can change**."

Exercise:

The next time that you observe yourself judging someone immediately offer them a **thought prayer** that reinforces their potential. Say something like, "May this person be granted new realization and new awareness in all areas of their lives. May they embody deep inner love to the greatest levels possible for whole life happiness from this day forward."

Your Notes

REFERENCE CHAPTER 43

The Effectiveness of Personal Agreements

Fun Fact: In Psychology Today an article by Heidi Grant Halvorson Ph.D reads, "High self-esteem does *not* predict better performance or greater success. And though people with high self-esteem do *think* they're more successful, objectively, they are not." So, how does the English dictionary coin self-esteem as of today, and if we as people are not putting ourselves at the front and center of our own values scale and priorities then where might we focus our greatest level of attention if not on the inherent worth of the self? *Merriam Webster* says plainly that self-esteem is *confidence in one's own worth or abilities.* Or in other words, *self-respect.* Perhaps, with a heightened sense of interconnectedness we might position ourselves to hold ourselves in esteem more regularly by how we aim to also instill that same very sense of inner personal value within the people whose paths we cross. Perhaps a true sense of esteem is reliant on the moment to moment inclusion of supporting other people's climb to greatness, too. Nevertheless, having a strong sense of one's best self, and a meaningful purpose, that includes the upliftment of others, is crucial to a whole path of wellness and health.

Questions:

1) In reading this textbook, you have now become more aware of the impact of your life's traumas and how you want to lead yourself to higher ground because and in spite of the trauma(s) themselves. **Increase your clarity** now by silently writing the following sentence and then speaking it aloud in front of the mirror: *"I realize that the sum of all parts of my traumatic experience(s) is less in power than the whole of my life in all it's meaning and it's glory! I realize that no matter what anyone has said, or done, I have already accomplish something great each time I make the decision to dive inward with the intent of realizing my life's genuine answers. And, so it is!"*
2) **Re-read number one:** Write for (2) whole minutes about what is easiest for you to say in the affirmation from number one.
3) **Re-read number one:** Write for (2) whole minutes about what is most challenging for you to *affirm, feel or believe.*
4) **Now, write your "why"** to number two and number three.

5) If you did list at least (1) thing for what is challenging about the statement, **write** (2) *springboard statements that lead you from potential negative belief* about our personal ability to positive assessment or judgment. (**Note:** *If necessary, see Chapter 41's worksheet for greater understanding on springboard thoughts.)*
6) This book's definition of success as seen on the bottom of page 238 in *Conquer Trauma Drama: Get Your Life Back* is, "Success is being able to think *when* I want to think, *how* I want to think and *what* I want to think. Success is genuinely knowing that I have nothing to prove, and then acting from that place." **Write your own unique definition of success that applies to your life,** including success in all of your major life areas i.e. *Relationships, career, friendships, romance, sport, recreation, health, spiritual, family, etc.* Make sure to write in affirmation style, you may **refer to Chapters 19, 20, and 21** in *Conquer Trauma Drama: Get Your Life Back* if you are uncertain of how to craft useful and helpful affirmations for this step.

Exercise:

Get your pen and paper out. Write at least (1) complete journal page entry about how you will feel and think once you have accomplished a top priority goal in your life. "Now that I have accomplished _______ I feel ________ and one thought that I can imagine that might be running through my head in this groundbreaking moment is ___________."

Your Notes

Closing Note

If you have delved into this book with consideration *and care* for *who you are today* then you are well on your way to becoming the master you were born to be. Answers are not always easily-identified, however there is always at least one *if not more* for every problem. Remember: problems are great. They lead us to solutions. Trust yourself through the process of your connecting to *all that is* as you work through this book. Consider working through it more than once; the experience that this breakthrough curriculum provides is like watching your favorite movie time and time again. . .Only *better* because the clips of the movie only become more and more rewarding with each and every practice run you do through these pages!

As you further realize and manifest your life, as you wish for it most to be, remember that "common sense" *is not common: everyone senses the world uniquely and differently.* **It is up to you to turn this fact into wisdom:** be compassionate toward people, *and foremost yourself,* if and when things get a little haywire in life. Whatever you do, keep stepping one foot in front of the other. No one determines your fate quite like you do.

Resources

The Guardian https://www.theguardian.com/science/2014/dec/16/cognitive-benefits-handwriting-decline-typing

National Institute of Mental Health https://www.nimh.nih.gov/health/topics/post-traumatic-stress-disorder-ptsd/index.shtml

University of California
http://ucanr.edu/sites/4-H-Fresno/files/191285.pdf

Brain Blogger
http://brainblogger.com/2015/01/24/how-does-post-traumatic-stress-disorder-change-the-brain/

Scientific American
https://www.scientificamerican.com/article/10-big-ideas-in-10-years-of-brain-science/

New York University Center for Neural Science
http://www.cns.nyu.edu/ledoux/pdf/daed_LeDoux_2015.pdf

Fast Company
https://www.fastcompany.com/3063626/7-surprising-facts-about-creativity-according-to-science

Huffington Post
http://www.huffingtonpost.com/entry/silence-brain-benefits_us_56d83967e4b0000de4037004

Live Science
https://www.livescience.com/44940-strange-facts-about-memory.html

Berkeley University of California
http://undsci.berkeley.edu/article/0_0_0/whatisscience_12

The Economist
http://www.economist.com/news/leaders/21588069-scientific-research-has-changed-world-now-it-needs-change-itself-how-science-goes-wrong

The Atlantic
https://www.theatlantic.com/science/archive/2016/04/the-illusion-of-reality/479559/

Scientific American
https://www.scientificamerican.com/article/negative-emotions-key-well-being/

Berkeley University of California
https://greatergood.berkeley.edu/article/item/power_paradox

Huffington Post
http://www.huffingtonpost.com/2014/09/30/love-yourself-science-study_n_5900878.html

TIME
http://time.com/3430670/self-compassion-health/

Newsweek
http://www.newsweek.com/science-making-decisions-68627

Live Science
https://www.livescience.com/19213-free-fate.html

Harvard Magazine
http://harvardmagazine.com/2007/01/the-science-of-happiness.html

Non-Fiction publication *Seven: How Many Days of The Week Can Be Extraordinary?*
www.amazon.com

Psychology Today
https://www.psychologytoday.com/blog/the-science-willpower/201112/is-there-such-thing-shame-power

Big Think
http://bigthink.com/videos/jon-kabat-zinn-on-meditation-and-thoughts-as-bubbles

TIME
http://time.com/56809/the-science-of-peak-human-performance/

The Bioneer
http://www.thebioneer.com/neuroscience-of-flow-states/

Wikipedia
https://en.wikipedia.org/wiki/Prefrontal_cortex

The New York Times
http://www.nytimes.com/2008/07/22/science/22angi.html

Scientific American
https://www.scientificamerican.com/article/feeling-our-emotions/

The Atlantic - The Psychology of Victim Blaming
https://www.theatlantic.com/science/archive/2016/10/the-psychology-of-victim-blaming/502661/

PsychCentral
https://psychcentral.com/blog/archives/2016/02/19/6-vital-facts-about-boundaries/

Springer
https://link.springer.com/chapter/10.1007/978-1-4615-4177-6_2

BBC
http://www.bbc.com/future/story/20150818-what-is-it-like-to-have-never-felt-an-emotion

Forbes
https://www.forbes.com/sites/quora/2016/10/21/where-do-our-thoughts-come-from/#5f3cc53e2ee2

Brene Brown
http://brenebrown.com/

New York Magazine
http://nymag.com/scienceofus/2016/09/you-should-visualize-positive-and-negative-outcomes-more.html

Scientific American
https://www.scientificamerican.com/article/meditations-calming-effects-pinpointed-in-brain/#

Masaru Emoto
http://www.masaru-emoto.net/english/water-crystal.html

Huffington Post
http://www.huffingtonpost.com/jim-sniechowski-phd/the-5-key-emotions-of-success_b_4103830.html

The Atlantic
https://www.theatlantic.com/business/archive/2011/08/why-good-advertising-works-even-when-you-think-it-doesnt/244252/

Online Etymology Dictionary
http://www.etymonline.com/index.php?term=power

U.S. National Library of Medicine National Institutes of Health
https://www.ncbi.nlm.nih.gov/pmc/articles/PMC2804629/

The Atlantic
https://www.theatlantic.com/health/archive/2014/09/understanding-how-grief-weakens-the-body/380006/

Psychology Today
https://www.psychologytoday.com/blog/the-science-success/201209/forget-self-esteem

Acknowledgments

There are so many people who have been solid contributors to my continued journey of creative exploration. I have rediscovered fun and fulfillment through the encouragement of my friends and soul family. Each of you have all encouraged me to put a stake in the ground, honor and challenge the darkness, and live in the light of my own positive personal potential. Firstly, to *Ren Jones,* who as a young girl encouraged me to start making lists of what might be possible if I dedicated my mind and heart in unison long enough. To *Chandelle Maldonado,* for sitting on the phone as I constructed the beginnings of this book. I experience you as someone who can challenge their previously conceived notions about other people, *and about yourself,* which places you in the top percentile of brilliant-thinking minds. To *Dianne Courtis,* thank you for being a support system on the other side of the world when I was traveling through Bali and planning my first speech. To *Carol Pearl's Designs,* thank you for making manifest my vision for the cover of my books. You are a wonderful freelance designer! *To Thomas DiGrazia, Anne Steffen, Dr. Karyne Wilner, Mary Shields Ph.D., Brandon Green, Svetlana Pavlova, Sales Samurai Mitch Harris, Steve Harrison with Bradley Communications Group, Mari Miyoshi, Alex Montoya, VETOGA Founder Justin Blazejewski, Lori Morrison, Dr. Faith Brown, Marine Corps Vet Michael Hodge, Dr. Bindu Babu, Dr. Felicia Clark, Luc Goulet, Julie Christopher CEO of Biztuition, David Newman aka Durga Das, and all of the many more leaders in the 21st Century who pave the way for more expansive, life-giving, thoughts. Finally, Stephanie Gunning, editor extraordinaire, I might not have reached this point of creating this Breakthrough Curriculum if it weren't for you teaching me new levels of competency with my first book. Thank you to Mr. Jump for showing the way by always doing your best nevermind who sees it or not!*

Readers, if you are facilitating a class or workshop that is healing and empowering in nature within your community, whether you are a teacher, leader, guide, facilitator, counsellor, coach, or psychotherapist and want to use this workbook to assist the progress of your group's members or clients please make sure to always use a waiver and signed confidentiality form in the name of best practices. **In general, a** "Liability, Assumption of Risk, and Indemnity Agreement waiver" and a sample "Confidentiality form" are best to give your community. Since this workbook invites physical movement and engagement of mental and emotional selves *as guided by you* it is advised to use both of these forms with your business, not-for-profit and/or community gatherings. *Please be aware that the necessary contents of each may vary from state-to-state, province-to-province or even country-to-country. Therefore, it is best to do your research before creating these forms.*

"Hate destroys, love builds: be a creator. Fear closes, love opens: be an advocate for life. Guilt stagnates, love permits: be a peaceful warrior. Anger takes away, love gives: be a foundation for life. A defeatist attitude makes its own bed while love has the power to design its very own house."

- Jo Standing (2012)

33708342R00090

Made in the USA
Lexington, KY
14 March 2019